Falling Into Place

© 2017 Antti Vanhanen. All rights reserved.
Devil in a Good Man, Maistraatinkatu 5 E 94
Helsinki 00240, Finland
www.devilinagoodman.com
Cover photo © Pekka Punkari, Fotoinfo.fi
ISBN 978-952-93-9765-5 (print)
ISBN 978-952-93-9766-2 (epub)
ISBN 978-952-93-9767-9 (mobi)

Man gets tired
Spirit don't
Man surrenders
Spirit won't
Man crawls
Spirit flies
Spirit lives
when man dies
Man seems
Spirit is
Man dreams
The spirit lives
Man is tethered
Spirit is free
What spirit is
Man can be

"Spirit" by Lewis Taylor

Contents

Introduction 5

The Quest for Truth 10

The Nature of Reality 37

TheSource of Our Experience. 69

The Origin of Our Problems 100

The Secret of Performance 123

Living from the Inside-Out 144

Introduction

For much of the last 25 years I have searched for answers to the question: why am I not happier and more successful? During this search, I have read hundreds of self-help books, taken dozens of courses, researched numerous forms of psychology, practiced meditation and mindfulness, studied ancient philosophies, and tried to learn various forms of cognitive psychotherapy and neuro-linguistic programming (NLP).

Everywhere I looked, I was met with promises of formulas, strategies, philosophies, tactics, and habits that would get me the results and excellence I was after. Yet despite my best efforts, no matter what I tried, I always seemed to fall short, unable to make a lasting difference in my life. And each time I failed, I felt a little more discouraged and judgmental of myself.

My failure to change lead me to not only question whether there was something wrong with me, but to rethink whether trying to improve myself was even realistic. Sometimes I wondered if perhaps I was lacking the self-discipline to apply all the strategies I had learned. Other times I questioned whether the problem was that I didn't really want the change badly enough. Occasionally I even wondered if I was lacking the intellect to understand and implement the strategies in the right way. All this doubting caused my quest for self-improvement to spiral into deeper and deeper levels of self-loathing and judgement rather than resulting in the happier, more productive, and better version of myself that I had intended.

I was just about to give up on the idea of anything changing when I stumbled across an understanding known as the "3 principles". This understanding – originally articulated in the 1970s by an uneducated Scottish welder named Sydney Banks – changed everything; I felt as if life and everything in it suddenly made sense. While I didn't completely understand the concept immediately, what I did understand was enough to turn everything I had learned about life and success on its head. And even though I was reading about the 3 principles (also known as the inside-out understanding) for the first time, somewhere deep inside I could intuitively tell that what it was pointing to was true.

This lead me on a new hunt for more information about an inside-out way of seeing and experiencing the world. My quest took me to authors like Michael Neill, Michael A. Singer, Alan Watts, Byron Katie, Nisargadatta Maharaj, Garret Kramer and countless others. Suddenly I had answers to the questions I had been asking all this time, and where they pointed to was the last place I had thought to look – within myself. It was as if I had been given a peek behind the curtain and for the first time in my life, I could understand how everything worked, why I felt the way I did, and why my results were what they were.

To my great relief, I found that I wasn't lacking will power, motivation, or intelligence. In fact, I came to see that there was nothing wrong with me. I was perfectly complete the way I was. What I saw instead was that I – like almost everyone I know – simply had not understood how our minds work and how our experience of reality is actually constructed. I saw that what had been keeping me back – as well as frustrated, anxious, and disappointed – was just a series of misunderstandings and false assumptions about the way the human mind functions.

Operating with a false understanding of how the mind works meant that no matter how hard I pushed myself, I wasn't getting any closer to my goals. If anything, I was getting further from the truth – and my goals – the harder I tried. It wasn't until I saw for myself what was really causing my experience that I realized the futility of what I had been doing, and that I was free to step out of my predicament any time I wanted. Contrary to popular belief, the answer I had sought for all this time had nothing to do with trying harder and everything to do with seeing more clearly. In fact, trying harder was the very thing that was keeping me from seeing clearly!

The result of this realization was that all the anxiety, frustration, and disappointment that had been increasingly surfacing after years of accumulation dissolved as if by themselves and my procrastination problem quickly became a thing of the past. Without consciously "doing" anything differently than before, I was feeling happier, more creative, and more productive than ever.

To my surprise and joy, these effects haven't worn off but continue to this day without me having to practice or do anything to keep them up. If anything, these positive consequences have intensified the more I've looked in the direction of what is true. What I have discovered, and what this book is about, is that we are all doing the best we can, given what seems real to us in the moment. As soon as we see through the innocent misunderstandings that are holding us prisoner, we are set free of the imaginary burden we carry.

Seeing things clearly is the foundation of everything we do. Without a proper foundation, we are unable to distinguish between cause and effect, and when we can't see what causes what, our behavior is misguided. We are all trying to do the best we can, but because of our misunderstandings, we often end up unintentionally causing great suffering to ourselves and those around us.

Thus, the purpose of this book is to shed light on the fundamental misunderstandings of life so that you can understand for yourself – not only on an intellectual level but on a truer, deeper level – how our minds, and hence everything we experience – actually works. When you do, I promise you that most of your problems will simply fade away as if by themselves and you will start to awaken to the beautiful lightness and effortlessness of life. You will start to realize that life isn't nearly as serious, difficult, or heavy as you currently believe it is, that most of your problems aren't really problems, and that the things you stress and worry about aren't even real. And the few "real" problems that don't fade away by themselves will no longer seem as daunting and difficult because you will find yourself attacking them with fresh curiosity, creativity, and enthusiasm. To see life from within is to see it with new eyes.

Keep in mind that this book is about discovery rather than about learning and implementing. There are no instructions, strategies, tactics or routines for you to implement or remember to do later, because those only add to the clutter in your mind. Instead, this book is designed to remove the false notions that stand between you and the answers that you seek. As such, it is an invitation to wake up from the innocent misunderstandings that are keeping you from enjoying life and achieving things with more clarity and ease.

Finally, I would like to say a few words about how to read this book. I urge you not to accept everything you read without questioning it. The point is not for you to get "the truth according to Antti Vanhanen", but to discover the truth for yourself. If you accept my word or someone else's without first examining it through your own experiences, it's only second-hand knowledge, a belief, or a theory to be stored away in your mind along with countless others. Beliefs and theories can always be doubted. Keep an open mind, but make sure you validate what is written here for yourself by experiencing it in your own life. You are just as much an expert in the art of being human as I am or anyone else is.

This book isn't meant as a comprehensive guide or to give you exhaustive explanations on each topic, but rather to expose you to them in an approachable, easy-to-understand and thought-provoking manner. It is my hope that the insights will resonate deep enough inside you that you will naturally want to continue looking further in the direction in which they point. If I may, I would like to suggest that you read this book the way you would drink a glass of nice wine; with an open mind, without haste, and allowing the taste and the ideas to linger. Whether it resonates with you or not is ultimately entirely up to you.

Antti Vanhanen, in Helsinki on November 11th, 2017

Chapter 1

The Quest for Truth

Welcome! I want to invite you to wake up to the innocent misunderstandings that are keeping you from experiencing more love, peace, and wisdom in your life. Without our knowing, these misunderstandings underpin all our bad behavior, suffering, and lack of results. However, as soon as we see through them, we find our way back home to the love, peace, and wisdom that we all seek, and we realize that they have been there all along, just waiting for the heavy curtain of burden to be drawn back, once again revealing that which has been within us the whole time, just waiting to be uncovered.

These misunderstandings of which I speak, distort our perspective and prevent us from seeing things as they truly are. When we don't see things as they truly are, we often draw incorrect conclusions and make ill-advised decisions that usually lead to more confusion and suffering. Worse still, as we misplace the cause of our suffering, we end up focusing all our attention on treating the symptoms of our suffering while overlooking their true cause.

Although it may seem counterintuitive, in order to see past these misunderstandings, we must focus on unlearning rather than learning; to remove that which stands in the way of the truth. But what is the truth? Many people are leery of this word, after all, doesn't everyone have their own truth? How can anyone claim to know *the truth*? Rather than the traditional, simplified truth – or our personal truth – that we usually mean (i.e. the truth is what is true), the truth I refer to is how it is thought of in many Eastern philosophies that distinguish between what is real and what is illusory. Illusion is anything that is temporary. If it comes and goes –

even if it is over a thousand years – it is illusory, because it is impermanent. The truth, on the other hand, is that which is real, unchanging, and eternal; it has permanence. It is infinite and timeless. It isn't true just sometimes, but always.

To illustrate this difference, consider a coin. Viewed from one angle, we can say it is round. From another angle, we would say it is a long, thin rectangle. Both perspectives are equally true but neither one is the truth. What this simple example points to is that what is true for one person may differ from what is true for another simply based on from which perspective it is viewed. Compare this with what is always true, like the law of gravity which applies to everything and everyone without prejudice. It makes no difference whether you believe in gravity or not – if you drop something, it will fall. Your opinion, belief, or perspective has no bearing on what happens.

Perhaps you are wondering why this is important; why do we need to understand the truth, and why do we need to distinguish between the truth and what is true? Because without this distinction, we are only dealing with perspectives and opinions. When we talk about the truth, however, we are concerned with what has always been and will always be – regardless of whether we believe it or not. When we seek and learn to see the truth – or the way things truly are – we are liberated from the abundance and maze of perspectives that are sometimes true and sometimes not.

So in order to see the truth we need to realize that our mind distorts our vision and prevents us from accurately seeing what really is. The distortions that prevent us from seeing how things really are take the form of misunderstandings that we have innocently adopted along the way. They are beliefs about the nature of reality, how our minds work, and where our experience comes from.

Unfortunately, techniques, strategies and belief systems are powerless against these misunderstandings, because they add to the clutter of thinking rather than help us simplify and clarify it. Our task is therefore one of seeing rather than doing. Put another way, there is nothing that we need to do or fix in order to feel better or get better results. We simply need to see that we are already whole, happy, and mentally healthy exactly as we are right now and – perhaps most importantly – that we have the power to convince ourselves otherwise at all times.

The idea that we are already whole and have nothing to fix is such an alien concept to many that your first reaction may be to disregard the whole notion. After all, every one of us can point to things we could improve in ourselves and our circumstances. How can anyone argue that more money, peace, love, achievement, and choice wouldn't make us happier?

This is the story we've been told our entire lives. Some of us have even learned to take pride in viewing ourselves critically as a means of self-improvement. But what if we are wrong? What if fixing our so-called problems won't bring about the happiness we seek? Today's world is safer, wealthier, healthier, and more educated than it has ever been. It's better by almost any metric, yet people are just as miserable as they have ever been. In fact, mental problems such as stress and depression seem to be on the rise. Something clearly isn't adding up in our world-view.

The origin of the problem is that we remain rooted in the illusion that more is better and *there* must be better than *here*. Just imagine what a tragedy it would be to wake up at old age and realize that we had all the ingredients we needed to be happy all along but we were too busy trying to acquire, experience, and become something else to notice! To illustrate this point, consider some of the most common regrets people have at the end of their lives: to let themselves be happier, to have the courage to express their feelings, and to have the courage to live a life true to themselves instead of what others expected of them.

It's rather remarkable how different those regrets are to what most people say they want in their everyday lives. No one on their death bed wishes they had spent more time working or that they'd worked harder on their six-pack. Instead, they just wish they had been more okay being who they really were, because at the end, they realized how great life was and how much more they could have enjoyed it if they had just leaned into it instead of always fighting to change it or make it "better". But where does this disconnect between what we think we want and what we really want come from? Why is it so hard to tell them apart?

Perhaps the reason that so many of us refuse to even entertain the idea that we are okay as we are is because we fear that without constant pain and struggle, we might stop striving to improve our situation and our lives will become stagnant. The paradox of this is that we fear and resist change yet we are forever trying to change our situation. We spend so much of our lives dreaming of escaping our "miserable" reality that we have become accustomed to living and working from feelings of fear, anxiety, and desperation. At some point, we have bought into the idea that we need pain to push and motivate us to work harder and that if we don't hang onto this pain, we will somehow lose our motivation to work and hence never achieve the success that we seek.

As widespread as this idea is in modern societies, even a rudimentary glance at the behavior of children reveals its fallacy. Human beings aren't inherently lazy. We are learning, creating, and connecting creatures. It's what we do naturally. We don't need pain to motivate us any more than birds need pain to leave their nests each morning or grass needs to suffer in order to grow. In fact, isn't it rather obvious that we function better when we approach a task from positive feelings or a clear mind rather than from fear, pressure, and anxiety?

If you could approach whatever problem you are currently dealing with from a mindset of peace, joy, and abundance, it isn't hard to imagine that you would achieve very different results. Perhaps your problem wouldn't even seem like a problem anymore, but just another step along the way. So how can you get this type of mindset? How can you learn to approach all your challenges in life with a positive, peaceful, and abundant mindset?

The most common approach – and there are thousands of books and courses that cater to this approach – is to find a method with detailed instructions and then strictly follow it. In other words, find a good strategy and implement it. But how many such strategies have you tried to apply to your own life over the years and what do you have to show for them? For most people, including myself, not a lot has been accomplished despite detailed instructions, solid effort, and good intentions. The reason all the well-meaning advice, detailed instructions, and "proven" tactics don't work as well as they "should" is because rarely can even the creator explain what inspiration, train of thought, or insight lead to the specific steps. And even if he can, what are the chances of them applying exactly as prescribed to your unique personality and situation?

The Power of Insight

The origin of every goal and idea is an insight. An insight is our momentary ability to discern the true nature of a situation – a view from within, rather than taking the word of someone else for it. Due to their formless nature, insights can be difficult to communicate because one person's insight is another person's platitude. Our inability to articulate our original insights makes it tempting to skip that part and jump right into the implementation steps without realizing that the implementation steps alone aren't even close to the whole story – they're not even the most important aspect. Without the insight to make use of the instructions, even the most detailed instructions and strategies are limited in their effectiveness because they cause us to implement them blindly with little to no understanding on how our own situation might be unique. Adopting a cookie cutter approach to implementing a strategy often ends up doing far more harm than good.

What we need, therefore, is to improve our capacity

for insight. Insights help us see for ourselves how best to use the tools we possess rather than having to rely on mechanical and generic instructions that don't take our specific circumstances into consideration. An insight – or a sight from within – is when we intuitively see the true nature of a situation or thing. What makes insights special is that a single insight has the power to change our lives in an instant, no matter what our circumstances are. Consider people who have had a near-death experience whose lives were permanently changed in an instant because they saw or experienced something. In that near-death moment, they were able to see something that changed their perspective forever, and we can see it too – without having to push ourselves to the brink of death.

So I'd like suggest two ideas. Firstly, rather than clutter our minds even more with strategies and advice, I want to encourage you to look in the opposite direction. Instead of thinking more, trying harder, or seeking out expert advice, try looking inside in the place that is quiet and calm. The more we try to find answers, the less likely we are to appear, because our minds will be too cluttered to notice.

Secondly, don't immediately accept the wisdom of others (including mine) over your own, consider for yourself what is being discussed and make your own conclusions from your own personal experience. Ultimately, you are foremost expert in your own life. Don't outsource that to anyone else.

If insights are the magic ingredient for helping us see things from a new perspective, we need to understand where they come from. Fortunately, we all have access to a constant stream of fresh insights – we simply need to know where to look. The best place to get insights is from a clear mind. When we approach a problem looking for answers, we are less likely to find them because our minds are cluttered with preconceptions, expectations, ideas, hopes and fears. Answers seldom come in the form we expect them to, and when we expect to find a particular solution, we easily overlook the many others that are right in front of us. However, when we approach a problem as if we are having a relaxed conversation with a good friend and we take our time to ponder and explore the situation in a relaxed and open state of mind, we are more likely to have insights.

As we learn to see through the misunderstandings that have distorted our sense of reality, we gain access to more and more insights about what to do and how to do it in all areas of our lives. We no longer feel the need to outsource our wisdom to other people and can instead rely on our inner compass to guide us. This doesn't mean we won't or shouldn't learn from others – because we will and we should – but rather that we won't blindly rely on others to guide us. We can simply follow our own wisdom the way countless visionaries and leaders such as Winston Churchill, Steve Jobs, Albert Einstein, or Martin Luther King Jr have done. They all followed their deeper wisdom, which allowed them to make decisions and take action that may have seemed foolish and dangerous to almost everyone else at the time. After all, all the great bets in life are based on instinct and faith, because data and consensus will always advise against them – otherwise countless others would have done them already.

Thus, we are pointing in a rather unconventional direction – looking inside where it is quiet and calm for answers rather than looking outside for strategies, tactics and advice that will only fill our heads with more thinking. Much of the world is concerned with efficiency, proof, and strategies for getting better results. Unfortunately, what we are missing is perhaps the single most important component: the formless space from which all insights and ideas come from. In this book, we are going to examine this formless space in order to understand the foundation on which everything else is built. In order to shed some light on how this works and how it differs from conventional approaches, let's examine the different ways in which we can change and learn.

The Six Levels of Change

By most estimates, there are over 400 forms of therapies and philosophies in the world for improving ourselves and easing our suffering. The different methods cover every conceivable focus area, from dealing with thoughts to managing emotions, from solving childhood traumas to thinking positively, from gratitude exercises to mindfulness practices, and from neuroscience to neurolinguistic programming. Whatever problem you want to focus on, there's an approach for that.

So why is it that none of these methods seem to work for all of us? Why do some people get results from one method while many others try in vain? Why is it that we tend to only get results while we practice the methods but rapidly lose their positive effects almost as soon as we stop applying them? Is the only way to improve ourselves to adopt mental practices as daily habits and practice them every day, like we brush our teeth?

This is, in fact, what the majority of the self-help industry today preaches. You see titles like "Habits of pre-billionaires", "Tactics, Routines, and Habits of Billionaires", or "The One Habit Most Successful People Have" everywhere. Everyone claims their method is the missing link to getting you everything you've always wanted. But something is clearly missing. If we have all this information and advice right at our finger tips, why aren't we more successful and happy already? Why aren't the step-by-step strategies and tactics working?

To understand why conventional approaches seldom work and why we need to look in a different direction, let's explore the six levels on which humans can change and learn. Starting from the outermost level and working our way deeper inside.

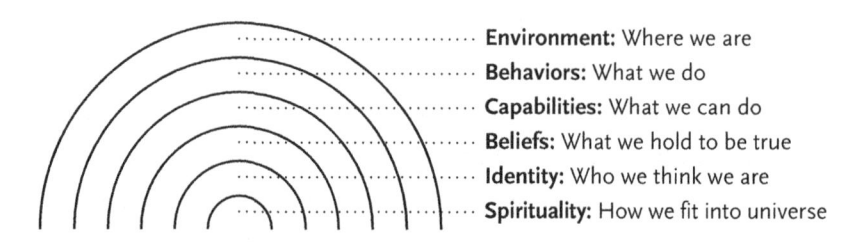

Environment: Where we are
Behaviors: What we do
Capabilities: What we can do
Beliefs: What we hold to be true
Identity: Who we think we are
Spirituality: How we fit into universe

PICTURE 1 - According to NLP, there are six levels at which we can learn and change. The outermost level is the easiest to change; the deeper we go, the harder it becomes to create change.

Level 1: Environment

The first level of change is the environment. You can rather easily change where you are to have an immediate impact on yourself – you can change rooms, go from your home to the office, or move to another city or country. You can go from a loud environment to a quiet one, from a warm place to a cooler one, or from the city to the forest.

While changing your environment has an impact, the change is usually relatively minor and short-lived. As the old saying goes: "Wherever you go, there you are".

Simply making your way to the office won't mean that you magically have the motivation to make those ten sales calls you should make, just like moving to another country won't magically solve all your bad habits.

Level 2: Behaviors

The second level of change is to change our behavior. The logic is deceptively simple: change what you do and you'll get different results. But trying to simply replace one behavior with another is difficult, because even bad behavior usually serves some purpose for us.

Most of the world relies on the strategy of trying to replace one behavior with a new one using nothing but reason, will power, and a combination of punishment and reward. Unfortunately, as we can all personally attest, this approach isn't very effective. If will power was enough to stop us from eating junk food (undesirable behavior) and got us on the running track (desirable behavior), none of us would be overweight. Yet millions of people are overweight – despite the fact they know *exactly* what behaviors they should change.

What we fail to see is that something deeper is causing our unwanted behaviors, and until we can solve those issues on a deeper level, we will face a steep uphill climb to try to change our behavior.

Level 3: Capabilities

The next level of change is to increase our capacity to do things. Let's say you know a lot about the topic of managing stress and want to coach others so they can minimize the stress in their lives. Although you might be a stress management expert yourself, if you don't know how to coach people, all you are going to be doing is telling them what to do (trying to replace old behavior with new behavior) instead of helping them find the answer for themselves. Thus, to be able to help these people, you need to improve your own capability as a coach before you can effectively teach them your stress management method Obviously, changing behaviors isn't possible if we don't possess the capability to do so.

Level 4: Beliefs

Beliefs are what we believe to be true about ourselves and the world. If we have several positive, empowering beliefs, we are much more likely to take action and overcome adversity. Conversely, if we hold onto negative and limiting beliefs, we are more likely to retreat further into our shells and give up when things don't go our way.

Beliefs filter what information is let through to our

consciousness. For instance, if you believe that people are selfish and unkind, your brain will generally mainly present you with evidence of that belief while ignoring most, if not all, conflicting evidence, thereby strengthening your existing world-view.

The challenge with beliefs is that to us they appear as facts, which means we are unaware of most of the beliefs that are steering our behavior.

Level 5: Identity

Our identity – also referred to as self-image – is who we are or believe ourselves to be. Identity directs our behavior and actions, because all our beliefs, capabilities and behaviors flow outward from the identity.

In the 1960s, a plastic surgeon called Maxwell Maltz stumbled upon the role of self-image as a cornerstone of his patients' experience of the surgery. After counseling hundreds of patients and over a decade of testing his hypothesis, Maltz concluded that a person must have an accurate and positive view of themselves before setting goals, because otherwise they will get stuck in a continuing pattern of limiting beliefs. The patients who had a positive self-image of themselves found themselves happy and transformed by the plastic surgery. Those who had a negative self-image, remained unhappy and insecure after the operation.

Thus, on the identity level we develop a positive inner goal first as a means of achieving a positive outer goal.

Level 6: Spirituality

In the words of theoretical physicist David Bohm, spirituality is the "invisible force, the life-giving essence that moves us deeply or as the source that moves everything from within". Put another way, spirit is the difference between the living and the dead – a dead body may have all the parts of a living body, but it is the formless, spiritual energy that gives the body life.

So rather than being some obscure metaphysical or religious concept, spirituality is really about connecting with the very real yet formless energy that underpins all life. Even though spirit has no material existence, it is the formless life force that from which all our thoughts, feelings, and life itself stem.

As the deepest level of change, spirituality is about seeing how the universe works and where we fit in the grand scheme of things. It's about finding the answer to the question how things really are and why things appear the way they do.

Implications of the Six Levels of Change

By themselves, the six levels of change are merely an intellectual curiosity. It's when we examine the relationship between the different levels that a whole new perspective opens up. Here's how it works: if you change something on the outer levels, little else usually alters. But if you change something on an inner level, i.e. deeper level, all the levels to the outside of it also change. For example, if your beliefs about yourself become more positive, your behaviors will improve by themselves and you will most likely find yourself more motivated, happier, seeing what you used to consider a big problem as an interesting challenge, and choosing to spend time with more positive people. In other words, change flows from the inside out.

If that's the case, you may be thinking, why doesn't everyone try to make changes at the deepest levels? The simple answer is that the deeper you go, the more difficult and time-consuming it becomes to create change. Concepts like environment, behavior, and capabilities are relatively easy to understand, while beliefs, identity and spirituality are a lot more obscure and harder to define, let alone change.

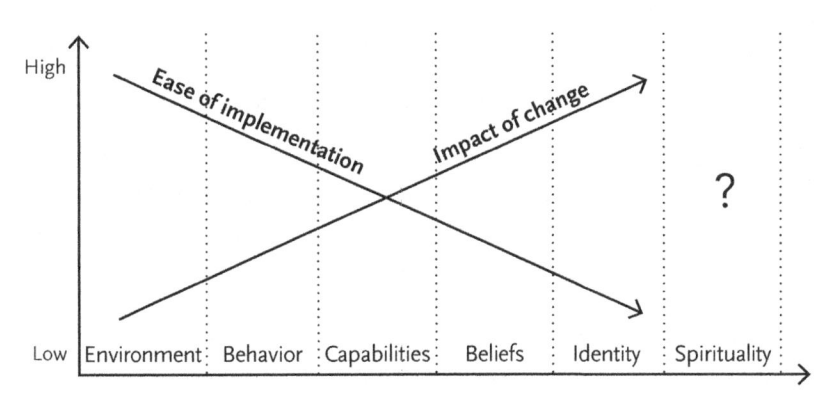

PICTURE 2 - Ease of implementation and impact of change run in opposite directions.

After all, how do you go about changing your beliefs or your identity? It's hard to nail down exactly what those terms mean, let alone know how you can change them. For this reason, people generally focus on trying to change their behaviors. It seems simple enough to replace old, negative behaviors with new, positive ones and it's easy to see the value of doing so.

You can see this approach being employed everywhere. In school, kids are told to be quiet and listen instead of talking and playing while in class. In society, people are taught to be considerate of others instead of acting only out of self-interest. In our personal lives, we try to eat healthy and exercise instead of eating pizza in front of the TV. In every one of these cases, we are simply trying to replace one set of behaviors with another, and our only tools in this are telling others (or ourselves) that their current behavior is lacking and that there will be a reward for complying and a punishment if they don't.

Yet despite all the motivational and manipulative tools mankind has used for thousands of years, changing people's behavior remains difficult and unpredictable. It doesn't appear that we are much closer to eradicating crime, traffic violations, selfishness, or unhealthy habits from the world than we were before. The reason for this – and it's why so much of self-help simply doesn't work – is that the behavioral changes we are trying to make contradict what's on the deeper levels. That which is on the deeper level always prevails.

Bad behavior is always a symptom of something else and it stems from reasons other than ignorance or malice. We generally don't smoke, drink, lie, cheat and abuse because we don't know any better or because we want to hurt ourselves or others. We do it because the bad behavior serves some deeper purpose for us. We may even realize how it's hurting us on one level, yet we continue to do so. Every single dumb thing we've ever done seemed like a good idea at the time. Every last one. Until we can either solve our problem at a deep enough level or learn to see it from a different perspective, simple behavior replacements are going to fail more often than they succeed. Here's an example to illustrate this in practice:

> Imagine you're a struggling salesman and you want to become better at your craft. You could focus on changing your behavior, such as learning to stand up straight, looking your clients in the eye, speaking clearly and smiling, because people like to do business with someone who carries himself like this.
>
> Almost everyone has the ability to master these minor behavior changes in no time at all and their results should improve. But to become a truly great salesman, you will also need to learn all sorts of other behaviors for a variety of situations. For example, how to deal with objections, how to sell to couples, how to sell on the phone vs in person, and how to follow up effectively. There are hundreds of different techniques, rules, and solutions for different situations that you could learn to become a better salesman.
>
> In order to benefit from all these new behaviors, you would not only need to learn and memorize all of them, but you would also need to be able to implement the right behavior at the right time. Copying a few simple superficial behaviors is manageable. Trying to adopt dozens of them and applying them at the right time makes becoming a better salesman start to look like rocket science.
>
> What if, instead of trying to learn and adopt new behaviors and capabilities, you would start by working solely on your beliefs? Let's examine what might happen if you worked on beliefs that you are worthy and that what you do interests and

helps your customers:

First, you wouldn't have to work on persuasion skills, because your message would be authentic and would naturally resonate with people.

Second, you wouldn't have to learn to demonstrate confidence, because you would know that what you do IS valuable.

Third, you wouldn't have to try to be like other star salesmen, because you'd know you are already good enough and you could be comfortable in your own skin, with your own style and method.

Fourth, you would no longer be so fixated on making the sale, because you'd know that other potential customers are just around the corner and this isn't your only chance at making a sale.

If you believed all this about yourself, what do you think would happen to your behaviors?

It isn't hard to imagine that your behaviors would automatically – almost magically – start to resemble the behaviors of a great salesman without you having to consciously change them. In addition, you would probably come across as more authentic because everything you said and did would be congruent with who you are, which would lead to people trusting you more and wanting to do business with you.

Changing on a deeper level frees you from having to learn and implement dozens of tactics and techniques to arrive at the same – or better – outcome. When you change on the inside, the changes automatically cascade to the outside without any conscious effort required on your part.

What the above example illustrates is that we can spend a ton of time working on concrete, visible things to improve ourselves (e.g. our environment, behaviors, and capabilities), but we run the danger of doing it all in vain if our deeper levels don't align with those changes. Whenever there is a conflict between the different levels, the deeper level always prevails.

The deeper the level on which we make the change, the more impact it has on our lives because the outer levels change without us having to focus on them. For this reason, many forms of therapy have targeted beliefs and identity as a sweet spot for change. However, both beliefs and identity are still imaginary constructs that stand between us and reality. Sure, if we believe we are valuable and the world is full of opportunities or if we see ourselves as successful and positive people we can make positive changes to our lives. But what happens when we forget to keep reinforcing those beliefs and identities? What happens when the beliefs that have served us well so far no longer serve us in the future? What happens when our identity is holding us back from a new deep and meaningful relationship?

Because beliefs and identity are fixed concepts, they often serve as limits that we've placed upon ourselves. We get stuck playing roles instead of living our lives authentically. Husband. Employee. Coach. Philanthropist. Democrat. Team player. Hard worker. Ladies' man. Feminist. Yet no identity is ever enough to truly capture who we are, because who we are is naturally always in flux and thus beyond what can be captured by any identity.

In fact, all the levels up until and including the identity level cater to and strengthen the ego. It is extremely difficult – if not impossible – to bypass the ego by focusing on things that are within the ego's domain, because the ego defines itself in terms of control. Everything it does is motivated by the desire to protect and strengthen itself. It relies on the familiar and is reluctant to experience the unknown. Thus, the ego makes it difficult for us to let go of the safe and the familiar and often prevents us from making meaningful changes to our beliefs and identity.

By definition, the realm of the ego is small, because everything it knows is based on what it has experienced so far, which is so very little. Thus, when we search for answers in the information and experiences we already know and what we can imagine based on that information, we are operating in a tiny sandbox. Our potential lies in the unknown and the unexplored. It's the place where insights come from and where we can go to renew ourselves. Exploring and embracing the unknown – the formless – is what we do on the spiritual level.

Change on the Spiritual Level

In the previous section, we defined the spiritual level as seeing things the way they really are. When we see how things are without our interpretation, we start to see how much of what we see and experience is simply a matter of interpretation.

Most people have never considered making changes on the spiritual level, because it seems far too abstract and obscure. How do you define what "spiritual" means? And even if you define it, how do you make changes to something that's formless, subtle, and difficult to understand?

Traditionally, work in the spiritual realm has been the

work of Buddhists, meditators, and religious people. And they usually devote anywhere from years to their entire lives to achieve enlightenment. Regardless of the method, the aim remains the same for all; to systematically try to strip away the excess layers of thought that prevent one from aligning with how things actually are.

All religions started out as expressions of formless and timeless truths. Over time, however, their original message was lost because people started to take the words literally instead of symbolically and the message became a social institution with its own agenda.

Spirituality, as it is defined here, does not require you to adopt any dogma or moral code. It is simply the acknowledgement of the formless energy that underpins all life. The more we are able to understand and flow with that energy, the more we naturally align with reality.

Fortunately, making profound changes on the spiritual level doesn't need to take years or thousands of hours of practice. Life-altering changes can happen in one instant without much – if any – practice at all. To explain how this is possible, consider the distinction between implication and application models:

Applications (or prescriptions) are how-tos, techniques, procedures, and step-by-step processes that we use as shortcuts to make progress when we don't understand the principles behind how something works. Most self-help, business, and leadership books and approaches are focused on applications in the absence of a principled understanding. Because applications are merely prescriptions and not insights into *why* something works the way it does, we are often left following the instructions blindly, not really knowing why we are doing so. We are like monkeys flying an airplane. This often makes it difficult to implement all the how-tos, because we have no insight into what we should emphasize and what we should eliminate as we apply the instructions to our own lives.

An alternative way is to approach learning by understanding the operating principles behind how something works. When we understand something first hand, it has **implications** that begin to guide our thoughts and actions. The mere act of seeing for ourselves how something works helps us make use of our new-found perspective and we begin to automatically align ourselves with reality. This allows us to resolve issues which once seemed unsolvable and lets us see opportunities that were previously invisible.

> *"In every systematic inquiry where there are first principles, or causes, or elements, knowledge and science result from acquiring knowledge of these... It is clear, then, that in the science of nature as elsewhere, we should try first to determine questions about the first principles."* –Aristotles

The application model is all about reverse engineering how something is done. While it can be useful in some select areas, it's not very useful when it comes to human beings. It's much more valuable to see for ourselves than to trust what someone else has seen, because their perspective will be different from ours and we can't know how exactly to apply the teachings to our specific situation.

To illustrate this, imagine writing a list to your grandchildren of the 10 most important pieces of advice to live a better and happier life. To you, it may be obvious when to apply your advice and when to make an exception, but would it be as obvious to your grandchildren? Would it be possible for them to see things as you see them or know all the nuances that you do? Of course not. Anyone who hasn't experienced, seen, and thought what you have will interpret your advice differently, and therefore your advice may do as much harm as it will do good to your grandchildren if they try to implement it blindly.

The final and perhaps biggest difference between the two models is that applications deal with *your* life, *your* problems, and *your* story, while implications deal with what it's like to be a human being. Your life isn't nearly as unique as you think it is. As you will learn in this book, almost all your problems are self-created hallucinations. They look and feel real, but they are very much imaginary – you created them.

A deeper understanding of what it's like to be human and all that comes with it can be incredibly liberating, because it gives you permission to let go of limitations, fears, and judgements that you've been unknowingly carrying with you for all these years. Learning to see what it's like to be a human being is learning to see how life, reality, and the human mind really work. Once you see for yourself why you are doing what you are doing and how you've innocently misunderstood the causality behind your actions, it no longer makes sense to continue doing the painful and damaging things you've done up until this point.

Seeing the operating principles behind our experience is like seeing the truth about something that doesn't have a material form. Gravity, for instance, can neither be seen nor touched, but we can see and experience its effects all around us. As soon as we learn the basic principles behind gravity – before we even know the word itself – its implications guide our actions in all that we do. We understand that objects will fall if we drop them, that it's going to hurt if we trip over, and that it is easier to ride our bicycles downhill than uphill.

The same implication effect applies when we learn to look past our misunderstandings and see the fundamental principles that govern our experience of life. Here's an analogy to illustrate this point:

> Imagine you are confined to a large underground building where there is no light. The absence of light makes it difficult and dangerous to navigate your way around in the darkness. Not only are you constantly bumping into doors and tables or tripping over things on the floor, but you also need to be aware that you don't hurt yourself by falling down the stairs or touching something sharp or scolding hot. Because the area is very large with a complex layout, you need to be mindful of where you are at all times and careful that you don't venture too far that you get lost.
>
> To be able to survive, there are various strategies you can employ. One tactic is to try to move as little as possible. Stick to the places you know and minimize the risk of getting lost or hurt.
>
> Another tactic would be to memorize the layout as well as possible. You start with your most immediate surroundings and then, through trial and error, you expand to areas further away. But what do you do if someone rearranges the furniture? You go back to square one.
>
> A third tactic would be to practice moving so slowly and carefully that you are able stop when you feel the slightest contact with an object before injuring yourself. Unfortunately, this

makes moving around very slow and requires absolute concentration at each step along the way.

A fourth strategy would be to get together with some of the other inmates and agree on how to make navigating in the dark easier. For instance, you might tie empty cans in front of stairwells to warn people of the drop, or you might take turns being on guard at the most dangerous spots to warn others that move in that area.

Each of these strategies is an application you can use to improve your ability to navigate the prison more safely and efficiently, and they all require time, discipline, and effort to bear fruit.

Now imagine if one day you were able to find a way to see in that prison, say, by finding a pair of night vision goggles or figuring out where the prison light switch is located. The implication of suddenly being able to see would automatically help you avoid all the dangers and move around the facility more swiftly. By seeing what actually is, there would be nothing for you to "learn" and no techniques to "apply" – you would simply see things the way they are and that, by itself, would be enough.

Obviously, in real life there isn't going to simply be a switch we can flick... or is there? Well, sort of. When we are able to see things from a brand new perspective, even a tiny glimpse of how things actually are has the power to change everything that happens on the lower levels. In an instant. Permanently. Once we see that something is fundamentally true, it transforms our thoughts and actions without us having to implement or apply anything – our new, more accurate perspective begins to automatically guide all our actions.

> *"Sometimes one genuine insight is worth all your previous experiences in life."* –Sydney Banks

A Quick Summary of Chapter 1

- When we are able to see what actually is, we automatically align ourselves with reality it is only when we get caught up in our thinking that we fall prey to the misunderstandings that obscure the actual causal relationships of reality the origin of every goal and idea is an insight and it's the guiding force behind any strategy or implementation plan

- We can attempt to change and learn on six levels; the deeper the level we work on, the harder it is to implement but more powerful it is in its impact

- Spirituality is the deepest and most powerful level and the home of transformational change

- Spirit is the energy behind everything; it brings people, animals, plants, and ideas to life

- Applications are instructions, how-tos and techniques to help you use a particular tool for your gain

- Implications allow you to see what really is so you will naturally align with reality

Chapter 2
The Nature of Reality

Do you believe in an objective reality? Do you believe that the world you perceive is real? Does it seem like others see, hear, taste, and smell what you do? This is how the vast majority of people see and interpret the world. We've learned to divide the world into "me" and "the world", a subject experiencing an object.

It seems obvious that the world outside us is concrete and real. After all, we can see it, hear it, smell it, taste it, and touch it. We can measure it, describe it, and document it. All the evidence seems to overwhelmingly indicate that there is a world outside ourselves that we all experience.

Where things start to get muddy is when we assume that what we experience is what others also experience. The way the moon looks, what cold water feels like, what a tomato tastes like, what fresh grass smells like or what a bird sounds like. We believe that our senses are like cameras and microphones that accurately communicate to us what is out there in the world and that we all experience things the same way.

However, the world we experience doesn't actually exist in the real world. Yes, there is something out there, but we have no way of objectively knowing what it is, because each of us are living in a 100% subjective interpretation of that reality.

To demonstrate this, have you ever observed how small children experience the world? They look at everything as if it is unique and new because they have no reference point to help them categorize or label it – everything is unique, weird, fascinating, and exactly as it naturally should be. Children simply observe what is as it is. Concepts such as right and wrong or good and bad simply don't exist to a small child. Naturally each child has their own innate preferences for things, but as adults help children make sense of what they see and experience by labeling (car, house, mom, dad, water, air, etc.) and categorizing (good, bad, right, wrong, etc), children learn to interpret the world from the perspective of an existing value and meaning structure (i.e. culture). The obvious benefit of this is that it allows children to adjust and function more effectively because they share the same understanding and language with the people and the world around them. And when children learn these concepts, it helps them learn even more complex concepts and ideas going forward, because concepts often build on top of other concepts.

Although labeling and interpreting things is a useful tool to communicate and make sense of concepts and ideas, it also begins to cloud our ability to see reality accurately. The more our mind analyzes, interprets, and labels things, the more things cease to be what they are and start to become what is thought about them. In other words, instead of seeing the world itself, we see only our interpretation of the world.

Contrary to what most of us believe, our senses are not like cameras and microphones that simply deliver raw data to us from the environment. Instead, our senses are informed by our mind at all times, and what we see, hear, smell, taste, and feel isn't reality, but rather our mind's interpretation of reality. There's simply no way for us to experience something in it's pure form. We've never seen, touched, tasted, or experienced something as it really is because everything we've ever experienced has been through the filter of thought. This is why we argue over wine, music, and art – we might see, hear, taste, and touch the same thing, but all of us experience it differently.

Our different experiences are the result of our mind that simultaneously creates and experiences our reality, and as a result, we all experience life differently. All our experiences are colored by our tendencies, definitions, ideas, past experiences, feelings, memories, hopes, and state of mind in the moment. Like our fingerprints, everyone has their own unique paint brush. Unlike our fingerprints, however, our paint brush is always changing; painting our experience with different colors from one moment to the next.

Of course there are shared facts of reality – for instance, we can point out a person, a tree or a building without any disagreement – but they play an insignificant part in our experience. The facts of life are basically a thin skeleton while our minds fill out the rest of our experience. Because our experience is inherently subjective, it means each of us live in a unique world of experience with no way of knowing what others are experiencing. For example, we all agree on what we mean when we refer to the color red. What we don't know is how each one of us experiences it. Our experience of the color red might be very different from each other even though we agree on the word (red) as it applies to the experience. Here's a simple thought experiment to illustrate this point; imagine there's a person who always sees blue when we see red and always sees red when we see blue. We would have no way of finding out that this is the case, because this person would have learned the meanings of blue and red according to his own experience. When we point at the color red and say "red", he sees the color blue but he has simply learned to call that color "red" and vice versa. The point of this example is to illustrate that even when we agree on all the facts and all the language, there is simply no way for any of us to know whether our experience of something is the same or vastly different. In fact, what you experience when you see red might be what the other person experiences by tasting something salty. Quite simply, there is no way to know how each of us truly experiences anything, because it's all created in our heads.

Another aspect of our self-created representation of reality is that we create all the feelings, meanings, and experiences in it. Reality itself is neutral, but our minds create all the feelings associated with it. There is neither joy nor suffering without consciousness, nor is there justice or injustice. Everything is simply the way it is. This concept can be difficult to grasp because we are so conditioned to associate certain ideas and concepts with particular feelings, but even an extreme event such as death carries with it no inherent meaning or feelings. Although we mostly associate death with fear, loss, and sadness, death by itself is nothing more than the end of life, which eventually happens to all living creatures. Death as a fact is neutral – any misfortune or tragedy we associate with it is simply a mental association we've attached to it in our minds.

The key problem we face when we rely on mental concepts to navigate the world is that as soon as we interpret and label something, it ceases to be what it actually is and becomes something else based on how we think about it.

Thus, death goes from being simply the end of a life to being a tragedy, loss, or heartbreak based on the story we tell ourselves about it. In the very moment we see, hear, taste, smell, or touch something and begin to think about it, we start to intellectualize it. And as soon as we intellectualize something, it stops being what it actually is.

Thus, at some point in our lives, reality has moved from the physical realm into a mental realm and we no longer know reality by what it actually is, but rather by what we think about it.

As our mind labels and categorizes things, people, and events, and tells us stories about what is happening, we lose track of the proper relationship between thoughts and events, and words and things. Our minds create our own unique, subjective worlds where we mistake thoughts and feelings for facts. And as we mistake our subjective world for the real world, we begin to fall further and further out of alignment with reality. The more we see the world through labels, concepts, beliefs, and interpretations, the less we see the essence of the thing we are observing.

As a quick experiment, take a look at the picture of the man in below. He's clearly an older caucasian man with a long beard and scruffy hair. You may also notice that his clothes look baggy and worn, like those of a homeless person.

But do you really *see* the man? Most of us just glance at him, because it seems so obvious that we already know what we are looking at and there is little to be gained by looking at him longer. "Yes, it's a sad older homeless man. And...?"

When we just glance at something and place it in a category in our minds, we are not really seeing its essence. We are merely confirming what we are seeing based on what we've seen and categorized before, and what we are doing now is simply confirming our pre-existing prejudice – whether good, neutral, or bad. In other words, we already "know" what it is and that there's no value in taking another look.

So what does it mean to really look at the man? What it *doesn't* mean is to categorize him based on his age, gender, ethnicity, attractiveness, grooming, or wealth – basically all the ways in which we have learned to make snap judgments of others.

Rather than looking at the person from the perspective

of confirming what we already know, an alternative approach is to look at him as if we had never seen another person before, with our mind wide open and free of existing prejudices and judgements. When we are able to see the person without analyzing and without pre-existing concepts, we begin to see his true essence, to see him for what and who he is. This allows us to understand and relate to him on a much deeper level than our analytical mind is ever capable of. It is only when we look, hear, smell, taste, and feel without thinking and while being fully present that we gain access to experiencing the true essence of something or someone.

There is infinitely more to the true essence of a person (or indeed anything) than any label or concept can capture. To use a label is to only see a label, and this is to miss its true dynamic, living, and ever-changing essence – the essence of life itself.

The Nature of Our Minds

To understand why our mind distorts reality this way, we need to examine the nature of the human mind. Obviously, there is great benefit to labeling, interpreting, and conceptualizing things because they are extremely convenient and powerful shortcuts that help us make sense of the world and communicate concepts and ideas with others. Modern civilization would practically collapse if we didn't have words and concepts that we agree on. But the nature of the dilemma goes far beyond convenience.

We are fundamentally incapable of perceiving reality as

it really is because each of our five senses – which are the tools that we use to perceive and understand our surroundings – is so severely constrained. For instance, we are only capable of perceiving light at wavelengths between 390 and 750 nanometers. All light outside this frequency is invisible to us. Our hearing is similarly limited, as we are only able to hear sounds between 20 and 20,000 hertz. Each of our five senses is inherently limited compared to many other species.

Our ability to perceive reality is further constrained by the senses that we lack. For instance, some species have a magnetic sense that enables them to orient in specific directions and navigate for long distances, while other species have an electric sense that allows them to navigate in conditions of poor visibility. Some species even have the ability to use echolocation to build three-dimensional pictures of their surroundings to help them navigate their surroundings. To make up for our lacking senses, we have developed all sorts of technologies including compasses, radars, sonars, seismographs, microscopes, and infrared goggles to give us a more accurate picture of the world. Yet the information these technologies provide us with is second hand information, which is obviously a poor substitute for our own experience. It's like having someone describe how warm the lake is rather than getting in ourselves.

What all this points to is that our senses are only able to provide a thin sliver of reality. And even that sliver of reality is far too much for our awareness to take in all at once. Scientists estimate that approximately 400 billion bits of information reach our brains each second through our senses, but due to the constraints of our awareness we are able to make use of only about 2000 of those bits. This means that at any given moment, we are only aware of 0,0000005% of our sensory input, which itself is already a tiny subset of reality. Furthermore, the 2000 bits that do reach our consciousness are interpreted by our mind, effectively ensuring that objective reality always remains beyond our understanding.

Here's a quick and simple experiment to bring the limitations of your awareness to life. Without lifting your eyes off this book, what can you see from the corner of your eyes? You'll notice that you can see all sorts of things without moving your eyes – furniture, lights, colors, people – things that you were completely unaware of just a few seconds ago. Next, what can you hear right now? As you shift your awareness to your ears, you may notice things like the refrigerator humming, people talking in the background, birds singing outside, your dog snoring at your feet or cars driving by – all sounds you could hear all along but were totally unaware of just a moment ago. You can try this same experiment with your three other senses too: what do you feel in the different parts of your body? What can you smell? What can you taste in your mouth right now? As your attention shifts through your body parts and your senses, you become momentarily aware of the sensations that were there all along, and then, just as quickly, you lose track of them again.

Our awareness is like a thin laser beam that only illuminates the area that it's focused on. Everything outside the beam remains in the dark. So what determines which microscopic sliver of reality it is that reaches our awareness? First, it's anything far enough out of the ordinary for us to notice. A loud noise, a quick movement, a sharp odor, or a strong enough touch. Second, it's whatever we happen to think to focus our attention on like in the experiment above. Third, researchers have found that we use our beliefs as the primary mechanism through which we filter the important information from the rest. But, you may ask, if our beliefs filter the information that gets through, aren't we only being "shown" what we already know and believe? In other words, is our mind constantly validating its existing view of the world, that the world really is the way we believe it is?

This may sound crazy, but that is exactly what is happening. Our mind is essentially reflecting what we believe to be true about the world. This is why people who believe that corporations are evil see evidence everywhere that this is true, and why people who believe that the world is a wonderful place see proof of that everywhere they look. So instead of accurately presenting what is out in the world around us, our minds are cherry picking things from a subset of reality that suit our existing worldview. This means our sense of reality is not a case of "I'll believe it when I see it" but rather one of "you'll see it once you believe it". In other words, our minds are constantly creating a self-reinforcing subjective reality.

We Are Incapable of Seeing Things As They Really Are

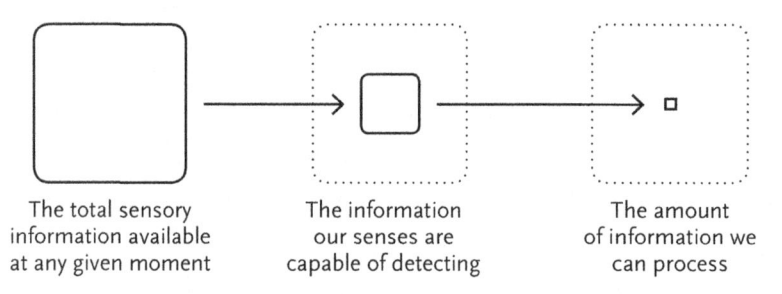

| The total sensory information available at any given moment | The information our senses are capable of detecting | The amount of information we can process |

PICTURE 3 - We are only aware of a microscopic spec of reality at any given time, constrained by the limitations of our senses and the bottleneck of our awareness. Note that this is image is not to scale and that, in reality, the amount of information we can process would actually be too small to be seen.

Another easily overlooked aspect of our mind is that it is always seeking some form of permanence. We live under the impression that permanence is a form of security, stability, and safety. For some reason, we seem to lack the capacity to fully enjoy the present moment unless there is a promise of more pleasant moments to come. This is why so many of us waste perfectly nice and relaxing Sunday evenings being stressed about the upcoming workweek and why we struggle to deal with uncertainty and not knowing how things will work out. As a result, we often choose an evil that we know rather than subject ourselves to the unknown. For instance, despite knowing how much we could benefit from finding new friends with healthier habits and more positive attitudes, we choose to stick to our old group of friends who only encourage our bad habits.

Our desire for solidity and permanence is perhaps best observed in the creation of (seemingly) solid structures such as self-image, religion, money, laws, rules, and agreements. But despite our need for permanence and our efforts to make life more secure and predictable, deep down we know that the world is constantly changing and beyond our control. The physical, mental, and emotional worlds are permanently in flux and no matter how much we try to control them, we can't. Thus, there is a conflict between our desire for permanence and reality's impermanence.

The result of all this is that we live in a world of labels and interpretations, unable to see past them, incapable of seeing the living, breathing reality beneath them. We are not aligned with reality because we cannot see reality. We are like blind men stumbling around, innocently bumping into things we cannot see and avoiding things that aren't there. It is thus our inability to see what is and our resulting inability to align with it that is the cause of most of our suffering.

Things That Fool Us

By now we've established that each one of us creates and experiences a unique, subjective reality. Let's now turn our attention to some of the most common concepts that keep us from seeing things as they are: time, identity, and thoughts, words, and symbols. We are so used to these concepts that it doesn't even occur to us to question whether they are real or things we imagine.

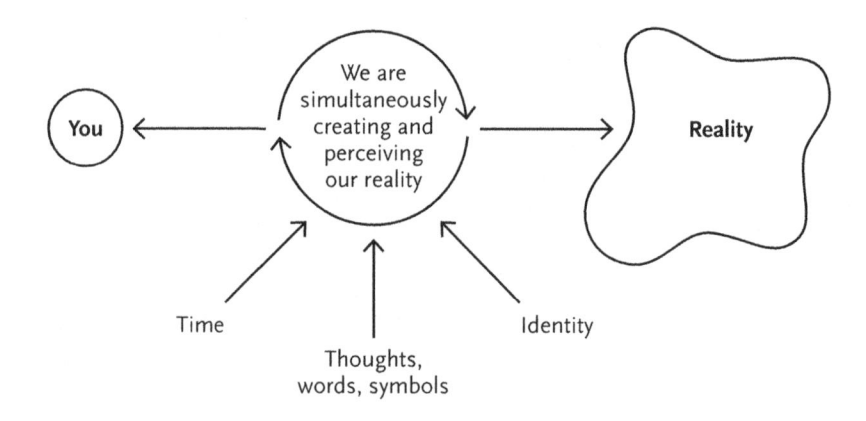

PICTURE 4 - The common concepts of time, identity, and thoughts and words are constantly informing our senses and creating our unique version of reality.

When we see for ourselves how these concepts stand between us and our ability to experience life more richly and directly, it becomes easier to let go of them.

1. Time

One primary advantage we have over all other species is our ability to remember the past and learn from it, as well as plan for the future. However, even though this ability gives us extraordinary powers of survival and adaptation, the way in which we generally use this power tends to negate all its benefits. As our minds divide time into the past, present and future, the present moment becomes but a hair-thin sliver between an all-powerfully causative past and an absorbingly important future.

Present
Past │ Future

PICTURE 5 - The way most of us view time is that the present is but a tiny hairline between the past (memory) and the future (expectation).

The effect of understanding time this way is that we virtually have no present, because our consciousness is almost completely preoccupied with memory and expectation, in other words, we mostly live in our mental realm instead of in the real world.

Consider modern society's obsession with the future; we are constantly predicting what will happen, trying to forecast the weather, stock markets, economies, sports games, technological developments, life expectancy, and so on. We're continually developing more tools and methods for our forecasts and spend more and more time obsessing about them. Yet in reality, the past and the future are nothing more than imaginary constructs. Nothing that has ever been said, done or experienced has happened outside the present. We will never have an experience which is not experienced in the present. Thus, we don't live in time, because all we have is the present, and it looks something like this:

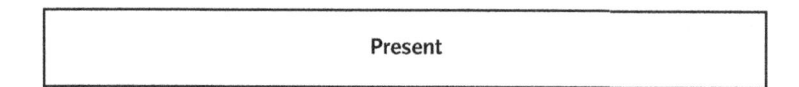

Present

PICTURE 6 - The only time we have ever said, done, or experienced anything is in the present. It's the only moment ever available to us.

Perhaps you are wondering what the problem with time is and what's so special about the present anyway. Why should I be present for things that aren't interesting or enjoyable? Why should I not think about my goals and how I will achieve them?

The simple answer is that it is of little use to be able to remember the past and predict the future if it makes us unable to live fully in the present. After all, the future is meaningless unless it is eventually going to become the present, and in which we are going to be fully present. Therefore, to plan and prepare for a future which is not going to become the present is about as useful as to plan for a future which, when it comes to us, will find us preoccupied with yet an even more distant future. In practice, this means that we aren't fully able to appreciate or enjoy today's dinner if we're focused on what to cook tomorrow, just like we're not fully immersed and enjoying our current holiday if we're thinking about our return to work.

As our sense of the past and the future has grown, our sense of the present has become equally blurry. This is reflected in our language, which is infinitely better suited to describe the past and the future – solid, unchanging things – as opposed to the ever-changing present. In other words, because the past and future are not happening *right now*, and are hence not living, breathing things that are changing and evolving in this very moment, they appear more solid and permanent than the ever-flowing present.

Our desire for solidity and permanence leads us to abandon our openness to reality and hardens our minds into belief systems by clinging onto thoughts about money, education, religion, science, and so on. Unfortunately, what we've failed to see is that just like the present that is always moving and changing, our consciousness also lives because it too is continuously changing. We – our thoughts, our feelings, our bodies – are just as impermanent as the present moment.

Psychological Time vs Clock Time

Perhaps you are thinking that being present and going with the flow of reality sounds great, but how would anything get done? Wouldn't we overlook preparing for upcoming events and spend our lives just doing what feels good in the moment? Obviously, being completely indifferent to time could not work. We need time to measure, sync, and organize our lives and to function in modern society. So how do we reconcile being present while also learning from the past and preparing for the future? The answer lies in understanding Eckhart Tolle's concept of two forms of time: clock time and psychological time.

Clock time refers to the chronological order of time and our ability to learn from the past and prepare for the future while remaining present. Clock time means setting goals and working towards them. It's predicting the future by means of patterns and laws learned from the past and taking appropriate action on the basis of our predictions.

Psychological time on the other hand refers to time we spend in our heads lost in the past or future, either through identification with the past or continuous compulsive projection into the future. It means that the present becomes a mere stepping stone into the future with no intrinsic value of its own. When we are lost in psychological time, our life's journey is no longer an adventure, just an obsessive need to prepare, arrive, attain, and succeed.

So how do we minimize the damage of psychological time? Quite simply, by keeping the past and the future in our peripheral vision while concentrating our attention on the present. This is, of course, easier said than done, and requires presence of mind to ensure that we don't allow clock time to turn into psychological time by obsessing about the non-present.

> **Example 1:** If you made a mistake in the past and learn from it in the present, you are using clock time. But if you dwell on it mentally and turn it into self-criticism, remorse, or guilt, then you are making it part of your sense of self and it has become psychological time.

> **Example 2:** There are a myriad of mundane tasks in our everyday lives, such as washing dishes, hanging up laundry, or shopping for dinner. The reason these tasks are so boring and unattractive is not because they are inherently boring and unattractive but because you've used your understanding of time to reduce them to nothing more than a means to a future end. You are thus lost in psychological time every time you do them or even think of doing them.

2. Thoughts and Words

Since most of our day is spent with our minds preoccupied remembering and expecting, it is no surprise that we have created numerous tools to help us remember, predict, and try to secure the future. From weather forecasts to stock analyses and sports predictions, we are obsessed with trying to predict what will happen.

Even before we had tools to forecast events, we created numbers, symbols, signs, ideas, and concepts to describe, measure, understand and predict the world around us. While these tools form an incredibly powerful and sophisticated system of communicating and measuring ideas and concepts, it also makes us confuse the world we describe and measure with the world that actually is.

To illustrate how words and ideas hinder us from experiencing reality, consider something as simple as love. To simply talk about "love" is to already be two steps removed from love. The first step is that the word "love" itself is just a sound we make that symbolizes the idea of love – it isn't actual love. Second, there is the exact meaning each of us gives to what we believe love is, which is not actual love itself. Love is bigger than what we can put into words or even fully comprehend, and whatever meaning we give it changes from one person to the next.

Thus, when we speak of love, we are using sounds (or scribbles in the case of writing) that symbolize our unique interpretations of love, not love itself. It is the same thing with every other word, symbol, and thought. From the color "red" to the concept of "love", we may agree on the language and all the external facts they point to, but how each of us experiences them is likely to be different.

It is deceptively easy to forget that words, ideas, and thoughts are merely conventions and things we have agreed upon to have a certain meaning, such as money. To paraphrase the great Alan Watts, money isn't real wealth because you can't eat money, warm your house with money or fill the gas tank of your car with money. In somewhat the same way, thoughts, ideas, and words are just "coins" for real things. They are not the real thing, but a representation of the real thing.

What makes this so difficult for our minds to grasp is that thoughts – like words – are circular. A word can only be defined using other words. A thought can only be understood via other thoughts. This means both words and thoughts are impossible to validate, because they are defined by the same mechanism that created them. Furthermore, when we rely on words, ideas, concepts, and thoughts to make sense of the world, we confine ourselves to seeing reality through a limited perspective. Every model, concept, and idea is a small, one-dimensional simplification of an actual multi-dimensional reality. In fact, any time we define, describe, identify, or think about something, we discard the vast majority of information about it.

Relying on concepts to make sense of the world is a slightly more advanced version of trying to make sense of everything using only numbers. Although a very skilled statistician would be able to create a view of the world that is in some ways very accurate using numbers alone, it is obvious that this perspective of reality would be incredibly limited and lacking all the things that make life a dynamic, living entity.

The bottom line is that seeing the world through thoughts, ideas, and concepts distorts reality, which causes us to mistake our projection of reality for reality itself. And when we don't see things as they actually are, we are unable to act in accordance with our innate wisdom.

3. Identity

Another common concept that distorts our reality is our sense of identity, or who we believe we are. We all have an image of who we think we are. One person might consider himself shy, intelligent, and kind-hearted. Another person might consider herself outgoing, social, and energetic. Perhaps you've even done a personality test such as Myers-Briggs that defines what personality type you are. But are you that person really? Just because the test defines you as an extrovert instead of an introvert, does it mean you are always extroverted? Of course not.

Like the rest of the universe, our moods, thoughts, and feelings are in constant flux. One moment we may feel shy, insecure, and introverted, yet a few moments later we might be feeling open, social and extroverted. When you observe children, you will see this fluctuation in behavior and personality. The reason for this fluctuation is that children haven't yet bought into the rigid idea of who they are, which leaves them free to express themselves in whatever way feels best to them in the moment.

Somewhere along the line, most of us lost our freedom to be and express who we are in the moment. We started to view ourselves as being a certain type of person or personality, and it started to interfere with who we naturally are, taking into consideration the fact that it can change from moment to moment. For instance, a person who considers himself mature, intelligent, and serious may resist feeling silly and childish for the sake of remaining congruent with his self-image. The same is true for the roles we play in our lives. When we assume a role in a situation (doctor, boss, victim, lover, friend, competitor, salesman, etc), it often causes us to behave from inside the confines and limitations of that role instead of based on how we truly feel.

Identity and roles thus often prevent us from following our natural wisdom and insights in the moment and force ourselves to fit inside the small and static box of identity. In fact, when you examine this more closely, you will see that your identity is simply your symbol for yourself, just like the word love is a sound that symbolizes the concept of love without being it. Thus, your identity may symbolize the role you play and who you think you are, but it can never capture the living, breathing, multi-dimensional being that you are.

So, what is the alternative? Who would you be if you stopped holding onto your sense of identity? What would happen if you didn't think about yourself? Would you stop being you or would you become freer to be yourself more authentically and fully in each moment?

Another way to poke at the concept of identity is to ask yourself who you would be without your story. Yes, there's a story that you've been telling yourself for much of your life about who you are, how you should be, and what you want. But what if you let that story go? What if instead of trying to stay congruent to the imaginary construct of who you are, who you should be, and how you are supposed to feel and act in various situations, you simply allowed yourself the freedom to be whoever it is that you are, in that moment?

Letting go of your identity doesn't mean forsaking your name, quitting your job, or acting totally randomly from day to day, but rather giving yourself the freedom to be who you are in each moment. When you allow yourself to flow with the natural ebbs and tides of what you feel in the moment, you are neither resisting nor forcing, which makes you more balanced and present in the moment. And when you are balanced and in harmony with yourself, you are able to connect with the world around you on a much deeper level.

When you stop trying to be someone – even stop trying to be you – you will find that your ability to respond to the myriad of challenges, events, and people in your life will improve dramatically. You will also connect to others in a deeper, more authentic way, because instead of trying to fit yourself in a box that you may have fit into in the past, you are now uninhibited to react and respond freely to whatever life puts in front of you. Once you realize your identity is just an imaginary construct that restrains you from flowing freely, you become free to step out of the box. Without the prison of identity, you can be whoever you feel like in each and every moment.

Leaving Your Mind Behind

Western culture is obsessed with the power of the intellect. From a very young age, we are encouraged – by school, parents, and society around us – to develop and utilize our critical and analytical thinking abilities. It's almost as if we are mining for a few very specific kinds of minerals from our brains while discarding the rest.

What we fail to grasp, however, is that the more we conceptualize, analyze, and measure the world, the more we live in a mental world instead of the real one. The more we train and empower our intellectual mind, the more every problem starts to look like an intellectual one. It's deceptively easy to overlook the fact that our intellectual mind is only able to grasp static concepts instead of reality itself, and the more we rely on our intellect, the more obscure our deeper sense of wisdom and creativity becomes.

It's not that concepts and labels aren't useful – they can be incredibly powerful tools when used correctly. However, we run into trouble when we start relying on them in situations where they don't serve us. When we apply labels and concepts unknowingly, it's like we are carrying a ladder with us long after we've climbed over the wall. The tool that was once useful is now just dead weight that is slowing us down.

So what is the alternative?

Instead of seeing the world and everything in it through the reality-distorting prism of the intellect, we can try to be in the world without analyzing, judging, or measuring it. In this sense, our challenge isn't so much to learn something new, but to unlearn old things that keep getting in our way. The question is, how does the mind, which is a learning machine, unlearn things? After all, the mind doesn't come with its own delete button that you can simply click to erase all the things you no longer need or want to think about.

As it happens, we don't need a delete button. When we

simply let go of what we know (and what we think we know) and allow ourselves to open up to whatever is before us with an open and empty mind, we become able to tap into the unlimited potential of new thinking as well as all the things we already know. Emptying our mind doesn't mean we lose our faculty to remember, observe or analyze. Instead, it enables us to utilize the entirety of our mind because it more accurately reflects the reality around us. The more still the lake of our mind is, the more accurately it reflects the world around us – thoughts are like ripples in water that blur the reflection of what is.

The big question is, how do you make your mind that is filled with thoughts, concepts, and ideas quieter? Our first instinct might be to try to force our minds to be quiet by telling it to be still. But that's not how the mind works. As anyone who has ever tried, it's difficult and energy consuming to try to repress thoughts for very long. In fact, the reason it's impossible to order our mind to be quiet is because the very voice that needs to quieten is the one telling it to be quiet.

Fortunately, the answer to quietening our minds isn't all that different from making a room quiet. What we cannot do is turn up the silence to cover up all the noise and make the room quiet. However, when all the noise is removed, silence is what remains. Silence is always there in the background waiting to be uncovered. Similarly, a quiet mind is always there in the background just waiting for our teller to stop its incessant chattering. What this implies is that a quiet mind isn't a state for us to reach, but rather our default state that is always available to us regardless of what is happening around us.

In order to reach this state, all we need to do is immerse ourselves more with the present moment, without judgement or analysis. As our minds begin to quieten down, we start to notice that there are gaps in our internal chatter. In the midst of continually talking to ourselves, we experience pauses, as if waking up from a dream. It is in these little pauses that we can relax in the clarity, space, and open-ended awareness that already exists within our minds. The quiet space of our mind is always simple, direct, and uncluttered. And in that quiet space, we are free from our mental world of concepts and ideas, and we can align ourselves with the reality that surrounds us.

You might be wondering what the point is of being present in something that feels boring or unpleasant, like doing the dishes. The reason we dislike boredom and other uncomfortable feelings so much is that we're not used to them – we are conditioned to pull away at the first sign of discomfort. Over the years, we've learned to misinterpret discomfort as a problem that needs to be avoided or solved. It never occurred to us to consider that the discomfort doesn't come from our circumstances but rather from our own thinking. So when we pull away from discomfort, we retreat from the actual world back into the safe embrace of our mental world. Each time we do, we reinforce the illusion that to be happy, we need to pursue pleasure and escape pain and discomfort.

It is only when we are grounded in reality that we are in connection with the very source that makes transformative change possible. Staying in reality may be uncomfortable at times because it forces us to let go of the very concepts that provide us with a sense of certainty and security, but in return it gives us the clarity, traction, and liveliness to move with reality instead of against it. The more we avoid and resist discomfort, the more energy we waste and the more planning and work-around solutions our lives require. Meanwhile, by being present we relax in the truth of what is. So when we don't enjoy doing something, it's important to understand that the source of our discomfort is in our minds rather than in our circumstances. In the case of doing dishes, it's clear that the process itself isn't physically painful in any way, thus the pain is purely mental. It's a phantom pain, created by our *idea* that doing dishes isn't fun but we *have* to do it.

> Here's something you can try out the next time you are doing the dishes: instead of trying to get through it as quickly and painlessly as possible, try letting go of all your preconceived notions of what doing the dishes means; forget how boring you think it is or isn't and simply immerse yourself fully in the process with an open, curious mind. No music, podcasts, radio, or TV. Just you, warm, soapy water, a sponge, and a pile of dirty dishes.
>
> Since approaching something that is very familiar to you with an open mind can be difficult (after all, you have subconsciously loaded it with meanings and significance over the years), here are some suggestions as to how you can approach it. Please note, this isn't a strategy or blueprint you should follow, but rather an example of how to open your mind anew to something you already know.
>
> As you begin, notice how the warm soapy water feels on your hands. Listen to the sound of the cutlery moving under water and the brush rubbing against the pots and pans. Notice the light reflecting off the soap bubbles in various colors and

angles. Find joy in cleaning each dish. Don't aim for efficiency or speed. Wash the dishes with a loving gentleness, as if each dish was a living creature that you are helping.

If you surrender to doing the dishes fully with an empty mind, you are likely to have a completely new kind of experience. For some, this approach has made doing dishes a beautiful, therapeutic moment rather than a boring chore that just needs to be done.

Even after you are done doing the dishes, you may notice you feel different. You are calmer and your mind is clearer. Simply by jumping into the present moment instead of fighting against it, you aligned yourself with reality and lifted your mind to a better, clearer mental state from which you are much better equipped to make decisions and take action.

Presence is Our Default State

It is quite a relief to discover that we don't need to do anything in order to be present. Everything we think, say, do or experience already happens in the present. It is only when we get caught up in our habitual thinking – remembering, projecting, or expecting – that we lose track of this fact. We are already present, we just need to wake up from the dream of our thinking.

There are many ways to wake up from this dream. We can practice meditation (waking up), mindfulness (not falling back asleep), or we can simply realize that presence is our default state. Sure, occasionally we will fall back asleep (getting lost in thought), but when we understand the nature of thoughts, we realize it's just how the human mind works. The more time we spend in the quiet space within, the more the grip of our conceptual thinking begins to lose its hold on us and we naturally start to align with reality. As our understanding deepens, it becomes easier to notice the transparent nature of our thoughts and we are no longer as easily swept away with each new thought that comes along. This allows us to catch sight of what lies behind our thinking and enables us to see more accurately how things really are.

It isn't just one layer of thoughts, concepts, and beliefs that surround us, but multiple layers in a variety of disguises. As we look in this direction, we begin to peel back the layers one by one, seeing past concepts and ideas we thought were fixed and true. Like peeling an onion, as we pull back each layer, we eventually get to the place where there is nothing left to peel. What we are left with is nothing. No concepts, no expectations, no right and wrong. Just emptiness. And although that may not seem like a big deal – or it might even seem disappointing to you – that empty space is the source of infinite creative potential.

This empty space is what's always there underneath all our thinking. It's our natural state. In the empty space, we naturally feel confident, connected, creative, resilient, wise, joyous, and alive. We make better decisions, connect with people on a much deeper level, and enjoy the ups and downs that are part of being human. There is nothing we need to do in order to be or feel any of those things, other than see past the illusionary nature of our thinking.

Most of us spend so much time lost in thought and trapped inside our heads that we miss what is happening right under our noses. We live in the fantasy of expectation instead of being in the reality of right now. We fail to live because we are always preparing to live. We can choose to either sit on the sidelines, trying to figure everything out and make only safe, calculated bets or we can jump into the stream of life and begin to interact with life in a deeper and more meaningful way. Each moment is dripping with magic if we just allow ourselves to be immersed in it.

While the facts of reality are all around us, our experience of reality is 100% subjective. To really see the world means to not think about the world but to throw ourselves into it. The world we see is the world we've made up in our minds. We then act in that world, trying to solve problems, escape suffering and reach goals without realizing that we made them all up to begin with.

The more time we spend in our heads, the more things become what we think about them and we end up wrestling with our projections of reality rather than reality itself. However, when we spend time in our bodies, we naturally minimize the interference of our thinking and are able to immerse ourselves with things as they actually are. By keeping our attention on the outer world, but combining it with the inside world of our body, we align ourselves more closely with reality. And the more closely we align ourselves with reality, the less pain and struggle there is in our lives and the more everything just seems to fall into place.

A Quick Summary of Chapter 2

- We all live in our own mental worlds of thoughts, concepts, and labels instead of in the real world

- Although we tend to think of our mind like a camera, it works more like a projector that is constantly creating the reality we perceive

- The most common forms of concepts that limit us are time, identity, and thoughts and words

- When we stop viewing the world through the limiting prism of concepts and labels, we start to align with reality

- Being present is our natural state and it manifests itself when we let go of our conceptual thinking

- By immersing ourselves in the present, our minds quieten and we are able to tap into the beauty, wisdom, and joy that are hiding in plain sight

Chapter 3

The Source of Our Experience

In the previous chapter, we explored the way in which we perceive a subjective interpretation of reality rather than reality itself. We saw that the very act of thinking – thoughts, words, ideas, and concepts – distorts that which already is. In this chapter, we are going to dive deeper into this idea by exploring how our individual experiences are not only 100% made up at all times, but that they naturally fluctuate from one moment to the next.

Most of us innocently believe that external circumstances, situations, and other people determine our experiences, our feelings, and the quality of our lives; that what we feel and experience is the result of what is happening to us. This is the myth that has been sold to us by nearly every book and newspaper we read, movies and TV shows we watch, and songs we listen to. This myth is prevalent even in psychology and the vast majority of self-help books.

But as real as the outside-in view of experience appears, in reality it is nothing more than a myth that has been perpetuated for centuries in the absence of a clearer understanding about how the human mind works.

The outside-in perspective that people, events, and circumstances create our feelings is an illusion that is at the root of almost all inefficiency, bad behavior, and personal suffering.

This misunderstanding leads us to try to fix the *wrong* things to improve our lives, and only ends up creating even more confusion and suffering. In order to best explain what this means, let's explore the different levels of consciousness that are available to us and where experience appears to come from on each level.

Level 1 of Consciousness: Life Works Outside-In

The first level of consciousness is the belief that our circumstances define our happiness. This is the level on which most people are for most, if not all, of their lives. On this level, our happiness and fortune is the direct result of money, friends, sexual partners, adventures, fitness, physical appearance, how others behave toward us, and so on.

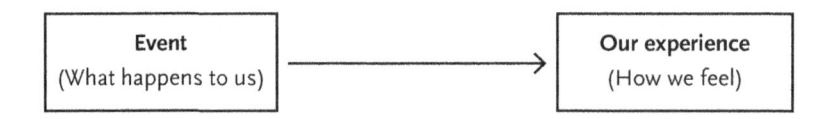

```
┌─────────────────────┐        ┌─────────────────────┐
│       Event         │───────▶│   Our experience    │
│ (What happens to us)│        │   (How we feel)     │
└─────────────────────┘        └─────────────────────┘
```

PICTURE 7 - On the first level of consciousness, our external circumstances create our experience.

On this level, we believe that our happiness is outside-in; where what happens outside ourselves directly causes how we feel inside. In other words, that our happiness is not in our control. The rich, handsome, famous, and powerful are considered happy and lucky, while the poor, ugly, and powerless are assumed to be miserable and lacking. In short, it's the view that our emotions are the result of our environment. On this level, an outside stimulus results in an immediate reaction. We are like rudderless vessels tossing in a sea of stimuli, with little or no control over our experience. Here are a few examples of thoughts and behavior when you are on Level 1:

- You are angry and swearing, because someone just cut you off in traffic
- You feel down on your luck and depressed, because others seem to be having more fun and making more progress in their lives
- You feel ecstatic and energetic because your team just won the championship
- You can't sleep, because your heart is pounding from the anticipation of being on a beach drinking frozen margaritas in two days

In each of these examples, what we feel on the inside seems like a direct emotional result to an outside event. Let's assume for a moment that this is true. How should we deal with our feelings under these circumstances? When our experience appears to be the product of our external environment, in order to feel in control, the only logical strategy is to try to control that environment to make ourselves feel happier and safer. In practice, this need to control our environment often manifests itself in a number of negative behaviors. To make the world the way that makes us feel good, we tend to:

- Judge and label things as either good or bad, right or wrong – this includes things, companies, and people (including ourselves)
- Try to influence, control, or manipulate how others think and behave so that situations play out according to our preferences
- Place far too much weight on the outcome of things – how a game of tennis plays out, whether we get that promotion, or whether the person we like likes us back all become of huge importance
- Resort to lying and cheating, because if the outcome is what matters, then the end justifies the means
- Justify our actions based on what has happened to us in the past

When we observe the actions of a person who is at the first level of consciousness, we easily notice how anxious, moody, and quick to judge this type of person tends to be. The reason for this is that they find themselves caught in an unwinnable battle of trying to control the outside world in order to feel good on the inside.

The limitation of this approach is rather obvious – the external world can never be controlled, no matter how hard we try. People won't bend to our every whim, we can't control outcomes no matter how hard we prepare or try, and things are constantly happening that are beyond our control.

As long as we continue to believe that people, events, and circumstances cause our feelings, our only logical course of action is to try to control the world around us with even more effort and guile. But because the deck is irreparably stacked against such an approach, trying to control a world that cannot be controlled inevitably leads to anxiety, frustration, exhaustion, and finally failure. Understanding this truth opens the door to the next level of consciousness.

Level 2 of Consciousness: Empowered Outside-In

On the second level of consciousness, we begin to become aware that a stimulus doesn't need to lead to an immediate and automatic reaction, that there is in fact a gap – a space or moment – between the stimulus and the reaction. It is inside this space that we can consciously choose our reaction. We begin to see that although we usually cannot choose what happens to us – after all, life is random and outside our control – we *can* choose our response to it.

From this perspective, life is 5% what happens to us and 95% how we react to it. This is a powerful insight, because it appears to free us from being a victim of circumstance and puts us in charge of our lives.

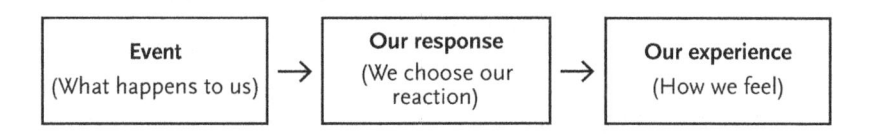

| Event (What happens to us) | → | Our response (We choose our reaction) | → | Our experience (How we feel) |

PICTURE 8 - On the second level of consciousness, our experience appears to be the result of how we react to outside events.

The vast majority of psychology and self-help books and courses are rooted in this perspective, because it recognizes the power of the mind in our experience and offers concrete, actionable steps out of our misery by steering us toward positive and empowering thoughts and away from negative and destructive ones. This approach has given birth to concepts such as positive thinking, working harder, visualizing the goal, and so on. Each of these approaches is focused on an attempt to control or influence our thinking and manage our feelings.

Trying to control our mental state leads us to adopt practices, rules, and routines to help control our experience and performance, as well as of those around us. Meditating for 20 minutes every morning, writing down our goals for the day, and talking positively to ourselves before a big meeting are just a few examples of behaviors we start doing to stay on top of our mental game. While there's no question that doing these things can have a positive impact on our behavior and results as long as we keep doing them, the strategy of controlling our response ignores one vital fact: *We cannot control our thoughts.*

If you doubt this to be true, just close your eyes for a moment and try not to think about anything. What you will inevitably find is that it's only a matter of seconds before you catch yourself thinking about something. The reason for this is not that you aren't skilled or disciplined enough to control your mind, but rather that it is the nature of the human mind to constantly think. Our brains are constantly generating new thoughts and it's a process that we have precious little control over. Some of those thoughts are positive and constructive, while others are negative and destructive. Some are useful, some are harmful, and some are irrelevant. This is simply the nature of the mind. Thoughts are much like a river, constantly streaming into our consciousness, influenced and molded by our environment. But as long as we cling on to the false belief that we should be capable of controlling our thoughts and feelings, we are setting ourselves up for failure; thoughts are beyond our control. And every time we fail, we become more critical and judgmental of ourselves, only further exacerbating our suffering.

It is not only impossible to control our thoughts and feelings, it's also counterproductive. When we cling onto positive thoughts or resist negative ones, we are interfering with the natural flow of our thinking. We don't realize that our minds work most effectively when we don't interfere with the process that automatically self-corrects. To make matters worse, whatever thoughts we resist, we often end up supercharging them through the sheer energy we pour into resisting them. As the saying goes: "Energy flows where attention goes, and that's what grows."

The problem with trying to control our thoughts is akin to trying to control our circumstances: we end up spending a lot of time and energy attempting to control things that simply cannot be controlled. In both approaches, our strategy is to improve our experience of life by controlling a specific factor. On the first level of consciousness, we try to control our circumstances. On the second level, we try to control our internal world. In other words, we go from blaming others to blaming ourselves.

The problem with outside-in approaches is that we cannot control our thoughts any more than we can control our circumstances. Once we understand this fatal flaw in these approaches, our minds are opened up to consider a more truthful explanation about the source our experience. This brings us to the third level of consciousness.

Level 3 of Consciousness: Inside-Out

If happiness cannot be captured by controlling our circumstances or our thoughts, where does it come from? Indeed, where do any of our feelings come from? These are such fundamental questions, yet few of us have ever stopped to consider them. After all, it has always seemed so obvious that our experience is the result of the people, events, and circumstances in our lives. By now, I hope you are at least beginning to doubt the validity of this premise.

Consider what would happen if the external world wasn't the source of our experience. How would our lives change if we saw that our reality is actually created from within ourselves and then projected onto the outside world? This may seem like the plot of a science fiction film, but it isn't. Rather than ask you to blindly accept this premise as true, let's explore this idea so that you can hopefully catch a glimpse of its truth yourself.

At first glance, it really does appear that our feelings result from the people, events, and circumstances that surround us. If we are happy, it really looks like we are doing things right – we have the right partner, the right friends, the right job, the right vacations, enough money, and so on. And if we are unhappy, anxious, or envious, it seems like we must be doing something wrong – our relationship is lacking, our job isn't satisfying or we don't have enough money in our bank account. It appears these events are the direct cause of our feelings.

But when we investigate a little deeper, we notice that we feel differently about the events, people, and circumstances at different times, even when nothing on the outside has changed. Can you recall being worried or anxious about something and racking your brain trying to figure out a solution, only to realize a few minutes, hours or days later that you can no longer remember what you were so anxious about? That isn't a glitch in the system – that's simply the way in which our minds create our experience from moment to moment.

If outside circumstances did actually cause our feelings, wouldn't our feelings stay consistent as long as the outside circumstances do? When we examine our experiences, however, we find that our feelings about various situations – no matter how serious or real they might appear in the moment – change much faster than the situations themselves. Here are a few more examples to illustrate this point:

- You are tossing and turning and unable to sleep because you are concerned about your financial situation, yet the very next morning you feel relaxed and clear-headed about the same situation – even though nothing in your finances has changed over the course of the night.

- You are so angry at your husband that you feel like throwing the remote control at his head, yet the next morning you might struggle to remember why you were so upset and instead view him with love and understanding even though he didn't change anything about his behavior.

- The party you are at seems boring and superficial one moment, yet ten minutes later you are thoroughly enjoying yourself and the company around you.

- One moment, you feel so happy and alive as you listen to your favorite song. Later that day, the same song has virtually no impact on you.

The facts of our lives are what they are – our bank balance, our body, our relationships is what it is – yet depending on our thinking in the moment, each of them can seem like more than enough or seriously insufficient. Our feelings are constantly changing, regardless of our external circumstances. The reason for this is that we all live in the feeling of our thinking and not in the feeling of our circumstances. Allow me to repeat myself: *We all live in the feeling of our thinking and not in the feeling of our circumstances.*

When most people first hear this, they assume it means "circumstance + thought = experience". In other words, they believe that it's our thinking *about* something that makes it appear the way it does. But this is to miss a vital point: our circumstances have zero influence over our experience. Circumstances and facts are merely a thin skeleton that our thinking fills to create the entirety of our experience. Our experience is created 100% by our thinking 100% of the time. So what the source of our experience really looks like is this:

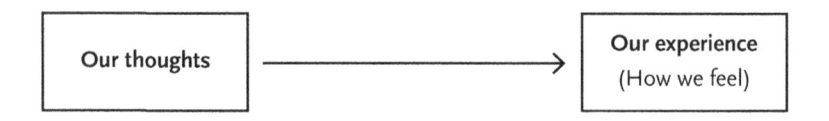

```
┌─────────────┐                    ┌──────────────────┐
│ Our thoughts│ ─────────────────→ │  Our experience  │
│             │                    │  (How we feel)   │
└─────────────┘                    └──────────────────┘
```

PICTURE 9 - The inside out nature of experience means that it is our thoughts that create our experience and not any event, person, or circumstance.

As we explored in the previous chapter, reality is *always* neutral – it's our thinking that makes things appear either good or bad, or right or wrong. It is our thinking that is creating our experience all the time, whether we believe it or not.

Experience: Correlation vs Causality

In order to better understand that our experience is the result of our thinking and not our circumstances, it's helpful to distinguish between causality and correlation. Causality means that one thing always causes another to happen (i.e. "X causes Y to happen"), while correlation means that both things usually occur simultaneously even though neither one necessarily causes the other (i.e. "X often happens when Y happens"). To illustrate this in practice, consider the following examples:

- An increase in ice cream consumption correlates with an increase in drownings, but neither one causes the other. This is correlation.
- Warm weather causes people to spend more time on open water, which causes more people to drown. This is causality.

Although ice cream consumption and the number of drownings tend to increase or decrease simultaneously, it's obvious that one doesn't cause the other. There is no causal relationship between the two. The cause is something altogether different – in this case, warm weather.

Similarly, circumstances correlate with feelings – for instance, feeling bad if we get fired or divorced, or if a project we've been working on fails. But these circumstances don't *cause* our feelings. If they did, we would always feel the same way when they happened, yet when we look closely at our experiences, we tend to find that our experiences fluctuate from one moment to the next. We don't have the same exact experience over and over again even in similar circumstances; listening to our favorite song doesn't always make us feel the same way even though the circumstances each time are similar. The same goes for drinking a glass of your favorite wine – it doesn't always taste the same nor does it invoke the same feelings or experience. Even something as simple and unchanging as the surface of your kitchen table can feel different each time you touch it.

The reason our experience sometimes correlates with outside events is because we have built up habitual thinking around certain people, events, and circumstances in our lives. Habitual thinking is the result of the meaning we have assigned to certain thoughts. For instance, if you had feelings of not being good enough when you couldn't do something when you were young and you believed that the audience caused your experience, you are more likely to experience unworthiness in similar situations in the future because it is now a learned response. When we believe something causes us to feel a certain way, we give it power over our feelings. The event's relationship to our feelings may *appear* causal, but it isn't. The moment we forget to engage in our negative, habitual thinking, we are free to experience an identical situation in a completely different way.

What these simple examples point to is that our experience changes according to our thinking in the moment. Thoughts are the sole cause of our experience. Whether we feel happy, sad, angry or restless, those feelings may *correlate* with our momentary circumstances, but the *cause* is always happy, sad, angry or restless thinking. Even strong associated feelings such as phobias can feel different from one moment to the next. For instance, you might be deathly afraid of speaking in front of a room full of people, yet if someone distracted you enough from your thoughts by – for example, telling you to count the flowers on the wallpaper as you are talking – you might find yourself delivering a talk without the fear you were expecting simply because you are unable to focus on the thoughts that are telling you to be afraid.

In other words, happiness is random, ever changing and out of our control. It has nothing to do with the outside world. It is here one moment, gone the next. Happiness is no more under our control than sadness, frustration, peace, irritation, joy, gloom, or ecstasy. They are all there for us, all equally out of our control. And until we see the truth of this, we are stuck believing happiness depends on living a certain way and having the things that make us happy.

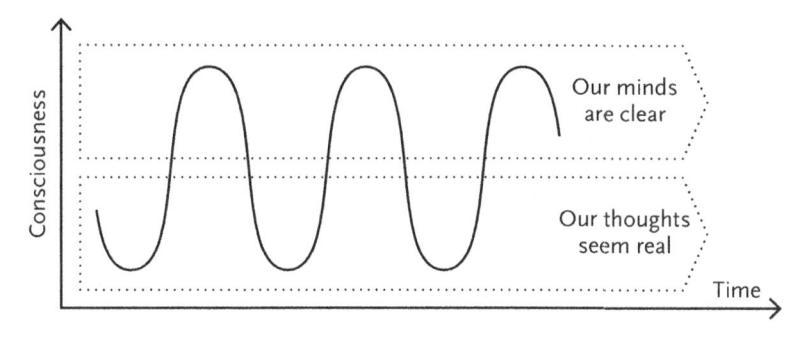

PICTURE 10 - As our thinking constantly and automatically ebbs and flows, our experience of life ebbs and flows accordingly between the spiritual and the physical.

The more real our thoughts appear to us, the more consumed by them we become and the bigger our problems appear. This results in more time spent thinking about them, and the more we keep thinking about our problems, the more cluttered our thinking gets until it becomes impossible to see the forest for the trees. When we're feeling low – when we're sad, angry, anxious, frustrated, or jealous – we're usually listening to the noise of our thinking, unable to separate it from our experience in the moment.

On the other hand, the less real our thoughts appear to us, the less they bother and consume us and the easier it is to let go of whatever negative or unproductive thoughts happen to be racing through our heads. We stay balanced more effortlessly and spend less time trying to fix our thoughts and feelings. When we recognize that our experiences are created via our own thinking, we are more likely to overcome obstacles and succeed. When we attribute our experiences to our circumstances – our boss, home life, bank balance, customers or coworkers – we tend to get stuck on the obstacles.

Perhaps at this point you are wondering that if this is the truth, why is it so unknown? Why are we all so unaware of it? How is it possible that such a fundamental truth has escaped us for so long? Why isn't it taught in schools everywhere?

One reason is that almost the entire world lives in the outside-in misunderstanding – our parents, teachers, and peers. It's impossible to pass on information you are not aware of yourself. Because we all have the ability to have feelings and the ability to sense the world around us, it's natural that we have connected the spiritual and the physical worlds in our minds – even though the two are completely unrelated.

A second reason is that our thinking happens so instantly (so much so that we are unaware of it) that it *appears* outside events really are the cause of our experience. Because of this illusion, most of us have spent our entire lives trying to create our experiences from the outside in, completely unaware that experience is created from the inside-out.

A third reason is that even when we are aware of the inside-out understanding, it is incredibly difficult to put this understanding into words due to its formless nature. Since 100% of our experience is created by our minds and not the world around us, there's nothing tangible for us to point to as the cause of our experience. Each person's experience is different not only from others', but also from one moment to the next. It can be a daunting challenge to try to communicate a truth that is formless and constantly in flux – just ask someone who's tried writing a book about it.

Once we see that our experience of life is created from within, we realize that we are solely responsible for our experiences regardless of what is happening to us or around us. Note that taking responsibility does *not* mean coming up with strategies and tactics to change how you feel, nor does it mean beating yourself up when you don't feel good. Taking responsibility means catching yourself when you are caught up in a bad feeling and reminding yourself that it's your thinking that is creating that feeling, not your circumstances.

Allow me to repeat and elaborate, because this is an important point. Taking responsibility for our experience means when we catch ourselves in a bad feeling, we realise it's not because of any circumstance, person, or event in our lives, but rather, no matter how strong the correlation feels, we remind ourselves that it is our thinking (conscious and subconscious) that is causing 100% of our experience. This doesn't necessarily remove our bad feelings instantly, but it does prevent us from lashing out at others or blaming them for our feelings and thereby causing even more damage. The less we interfere with our experience by getting caught up in our thinking, the quicker we will have access to fresh, new thinking and our bad feelings are able to pass through. When you think about it, it's rather obvious that we are more likely to have a constructive conversation with someone when we aren't coming from a place of anger, fear, or frustration, but rather a place of balance, peace, and curiosity.

It's also important to understand that our feelings are not only the result of our conscious thinking – it's the total sum of our conscious and subconscious thinking. Our subconscious thinking is essentially where our moods come from. Moods come and go without any clear pattern or cause because of the subconscious thinking that's going on underneath. Whether we jump out of bed motivated and ready to embrace the challenges of the day or we just want to crawl right back under the covers and do nothing but watch Netflix all day, the cause is our subconscious thinking, not whatever else is going on in our lives.

What It Means To Look Inside

If everything is made of thought, and facts and circumstances are neutral, then does it mean that nothing really matters? Well, yes and no. While anything anyone considers good, bad, important, or unimportant is ultimately the result of their thinking and not the inherent objective quality of the thing itself, feelings are what make living not only worthwhile, but also possible. Every living creature is ultimately guided by emotion – each of us comes with an inbuilt, natural intelligence that guides us to survive, reproduce, and thrive without us having to consciously think about it.

Life would hold little meaning if it wasn't for our feelings, and just because we see the thought-feeling connection it doesn't by any means imply that we should let go of everything we love and enjoy in our lives. Quite the contrary – it's the outside-in illusion that gives life much of its magic. It's really only when we find ourselves veering off course (i.e. feeling bad or engaging in destructive behaviors) that we need to remind ourselves of this connection. This allows us to wake up from the dream of our thinking and returns our mind back to balance from where we can see things more clearly and accurately.

For instance, there will be consequences if we can't pay our rent next month, just like we are likely to remain overweight if we don't reduce our calorie intake and start exercising more. That's just the way things are. But how we feel about them is not an inherent quality of those circumstances. When we see that the worry of paying our rent as a means to feel secure or the depression of our never-ending quest to lose weight as a means to feel good about ourselves are merely the stories we've attached to our circumstances, we become free to let them go. Worry, stress, and depression are all just psychological deadweight that we unnecessarily carry on our shoulders. That deadweight comes from the stories we tell ourselves about our particular circumstances, not how things actually are. While simply letting go of the psychological deadweight doesn't necessarily solve the issue, it will allow you to see things more clearly and free your mind to find the best way forward.

Once we realize that the psychological weight we are carrying is imaginary, we no longer need to come up with strategies to cope with the burden of the additional and unnecessary weight. We can simply let it go. After all, the weight we've been carrying all this time really *is* just thought, and all thoughts are transient and temporary by nature.

There's a common misconception that stress and worry are necessary for getting things done. We believe that we need to hold onto negative feelings to drive us to do things we don't want to do. In reality, this is just another culturally perpetuated misunderstanding; that in order to succeed, we need to suffer and put pressure on ourselves. But the fact of the matter is that when we are stressed, worried, depressed, or under tremendous psychological pressure, we seldom think straight or perform well. Getting caught up in troubled thinking also tends to cause a great deal of collateral damage in other parts of our lives. Someone who is busy worrying about their performance review at work is less likely to be present and understanding and more likely to lash out when things don't go his way.

When we are troubled, we tend to think the same old thoughts over and over again, only at an increasingly frantic pace. The more we have on our minds, the less space we have to see and think clearly and our capacity to have new insights is greatly diminished. It is only when we allow our minds to relax that we start to see clearly and often discover ideas and solutions that we couldn't see before. Worrying about paying your rent next month won't make it any more likely that you will find a way to pay it. In fact, it's quite the opposite. It's only when you stop worrying that you can give your full attention to the problem at hand, thereby gaining access to new ideas and solutions that, once discovered, might seem quite obvious. Similarly, having a demanding job doesn't need to be stressful. Stress is the result of stressful thinking, not an outside circumstance. If you leave the stress label by the wayside and embrace your job and its demands, you are just as likely to find that the job is fast-paced and interesting as you are to find it stressful.

All of us fall into the outside-in way of looking at life from time to time. When this happens, our thoughts seem so real that we forget that they're only thoughts and that our feeling isn't actually created by our circumstances. But when our thoughts sweep us away, all we need to do to return to balance is to remember that we are in fact feeling our thinking and not our circumstances. This allows us to let go of our troublesome thoughts – or, at the very least, not let ourselves get swept away with the drama and turmoil.

The Inside-Out Nature of Experience

Like all great truths in life, the more we try to intellectually grasp the inside-out understanding of life, the more elusive it seems. The closer we get to it, the less words we seem to have to accurately describe what it is. So don't worry if it all sounds a bit confusing still – trust me, I get it. It may take some time to sink in. Here are seven qualities of life's inside-out nature to reflect upon:

1. *Everything* is Made Up of Thoughts

Almost the entire world lives under the illusion that our thoughts are real and created from "reality". This includes most psychiatrists, mental health professionals, and many self-help gurus who attempt to ease their patients' suffering by trying to process their past or analyze and understand the content of their personal thought systems.

Yet in truth, all our problems and suffering are the result of our thinking, and just as easily as we are holding onto them we can also let them go. When we understand on a gut level that they're just thoughts and that they aren't "real", they lose their power over us.

Since everything we experience is brought to our awareness through thought, we don't need to analyze the contents of those thoughts as much as we need to simply realize that we are thinking and thus creating our experience.

This simplifies life a great deal, because it frees us from having to constantly manage our thoughts and feelings. For instance, when we feel demotivated or sad, we don't need to manage the content of our thoughts or understand where the feeling is coming from, we simply need to realize that the experience is 100% the result of our thinking and it will naturally pass on its own without anything needing to be done about it.

"The most important thing to remember is it's not underlined what you think – it's the fact that you think. Thought holds the secret to all our happiness, all our sadness." –Sydney Banks

2. Our Minds Work Only One Way

Whether we are aware of it or not, our minds work only one way: inside-out. Every person who has ever existed has created 100% of their experience from the inside-out. Not 99% of the time. 100% of the time. Everyone. Even if you don't yet see the inside-out nature of reality, your opinion is the result of your inside-out understanding.

The inside-out nature of reality applies to everything in life, even to such dramatic outside events such as being hit in the face. At first glance, it might seem to you that of course getting hit in the face is a negative experience. But is this really always the case? What about masochists who enjoy pain? What about boxers whose job it is to hit and get hit? What about accidentally getting hit in the face by, say, a snowball? In other words, even something as "obviously negative" as getting hit in the face has an awful lot of exceptions where the experience isn't negative but neutral or even positive.

This indicates that there is no such thing as an objectively negative experience – every single negative experience is actually a 100% subjective thought-created experience. Whether we realize it or not, all of us form our perceptions from the inside-out. Our thoughts generate our feelings, and our feelings generate our moods. As Sydney Banks was fond of saying, life is a contact sport. Pain is inevitable, but suffering is optional. To get a better grasp of what this means, let's look at physical pain. Even physical pain is created via our thoughts, because our senses bring our thinking to life. I am sure you can recall instances from your life when you've been in physical pain, only to have something sudden happen – such as the curtain catching fire – and like the flick of a switch you would all but forget about your pain.

As long as we are unaware that the inside-out dynamic is always at work, we will continue to attach our emotions to our past, present, or future circumstances. Our minds always have and always will work this way. The sooner we understand this, the sooner we can start working *with* the way our minds naturally function instead of *against* them.

Our perceptions and feelings are our thoughts in action, brought to life in our consciousness. It is impossible for us to experience *anything* without our thinking creating *all* of our experience.

3. We Create 100% of our Experience

Once we realize that our perceptions and feelings are generated in our mind, we stop seeing events, people and circumstances as responsible for our inner experiences. For instance:

- Being surrounded by crying kids doesn't make you feel irritated – your thinking does
- Being laid off from your work doesn't make you feel insecure – your thinking does
- Winning the lottery doesn't make you feel ecstatic – your thinking does

- Being overweight doesn't make you feel unattractive – your thinking does
- Losing a big game doesn't make you feel disappointed – your thinking does

Realizing that our thoughts create our feelings doesn't mean we need to try to control how we feel. As we've discussed, controlling our thoughts – and by extension controlling our feelings – is impossible. It simply means that it doesn't make sense to blame others or our circumstances for how we are feeling. As a result, we spend much less time judging others and ourselves.

This doesn't mean understanding the inside-out nature of experience will prevent you from ever feeling insecure, angry or depressed again, rather it helps you realize that you only feel that way because you have insecure, angry or depressed thinking. And when you recognize that your bad feelings are the result of your thinking and not your circumstances, your thinking begins to settle on its own without you having to manage it or your circumstances in any way. It may not happen immediately, but it will happen more quickly than if you interfere with it.

There's a real beauty to this process; we don't need to win the lottery in order to have the same kind of feelings, because all feelings are thought-generated and not caused by our circumstances. This means we have the ability to experience every feeling without anything in particular happening to us. As you will discover later in this book, this realization lays the foundation for a completely new way of being in the world.

4. Our Thinking is Always in Flux

Our minds are constantly creating new, fresh thinking. It's why our moods and perspectives change from one moment to the next. This isn't a mistake in our programming, but how the human mind naturally operates. We can have a totally different perspective from one moment to the next due to this natural ebb and flow of thinking. It's why we feel differently about our jobs, friends, spouses, homes, bosses, ourselves, and even world politics on a daily basis. It's also how we are suddenly able to come up with a solution to a vexing problem that we've been trying to figure out for weeks while we are out on a walk or in the shower.

All of our thoughts are neutral; as long as we don't empower them, they have no power over us. It is only when we try to interfere with them (e.g. by trying to hang on to positive thoughts or deny negative ones) that our thinking begins to stall and our mind is unable to access the natural flow of new thinking.

As you will discover later in the book, understanding that our moods, feelings, and perspectives are naturally fluctuating helps us distinguish when we should stay the course and when we should change what we are doing.

5. Our Consciousness Moves Up and Down like an Elevator

As our thoughts fluctuate, our level of consciousness fluctuates too. The more clearly we learn to see that our thoughts are creating our experience, the more likely it is that our mind makes a leap to a higher level of consciousness. The higher we jump, the more clearly we see things and the more simple and enjoyable life appears and therefore becomes.

We don't consciously get to choose to make the jump or when it happens, let alone prepare for it. It might happen suddenly, or it might happen gradually. When it happens, you start to experience life differently. It's not that our circumstances change, but because we've shifted internally, our experience of our circumstances can often change dramatically. It is important to realize, however, that just because we've made a jump to a higher level of consciousness, it doesn't mean we don't sometimes fall back down to a lower level. Because we will. We do, no matter how attune we are to the inside-out understanding. The jump to a higher level simply becomes the new baseline of our experience, and the higher our baseline, the easier it is for us to notice when our consciousness slips to a lower level.

The lower our level of consciousness, the more real our thoughts seem to us, and the more likely we are to blame others for our feelings. Doing so, however, only strengthens the outside-in illusion because the more we defend and justify our feelings, the more we cement their realness in our minds.

When our baseline consciousness is high enough, it is easier to see through the outside-in illusion. When our world, which normally appears bright, colorful, and enjoyable, suddenly appears dark, difficult, and hostile, the contrast makes it easier for us to realize that we are creating the illusion. In fact, when we go down to the lower level of consciousness that used to be our earlier baseline, we notice what a bleak and stressful place it often is.

Learning to see that thoughts create our moods and

our moods create the appearance of our world is the quickest and most effective way of snapping out of it. The more we think, the more likely our level of consciousness is to drop, because we get embroiled in our thinking, which spins faster and faster inside our heads. The less we think, the less clutter we have on our minds and the more likely our consciousness is to rise, and the clearer we see and think.

6. Our Minds Have a Built-In Design for Success

Just as our body automatically maintains and repairs itself, our mind has the same capacity – if we only let it. Yet most of us are very quick to react to the slightest sign of discomfort, as if we constantly need to be tending to our mental wellbeing.

Ironically, the more we think about our problems, the more feelings of anxiety, anger, and frustration we create. And from that state of heightened discomfort, the world looks difficult, unfriendly, and full of problems. It never occurs to us that our view of the world in that state isn't accurate or that the world only looks that way because we happen to be momentarily on a lower level of consciousness. In that state, our thoughts look so real to us that we forget they are just thoughts that we project onto the outside world.

When our thoughts look real to us, mountains grow out of molehills and we rush to fix those problems. The most common approach to fixing problems is to try to implement advice, hacks, techniques, strategies, and routines into our lives. However, all this does is further complicate our thinking, resulting in less clarity, wisdom, and insight. In other words, in our rush to fix our problems, we have just made getting positive results all the more difficult.

Behind every problem there are bad feelings, and our problems are simply our coping mechanisms for those feelings. The irony of the situation is that if we just leave the thoughts alone, the storm blows over faster and our minds become clearer.

It's perfectly human to be angry, sad, afraid, or a myriad of other negative emotions. The wonderful news is that we don't have to act on the thoughts that cause those feelings. We only need to see that we are living in the feeling of our thinking, and that fixing some external problem or lashing out at others is misdirected energy that will almost always do more harm than good.

So the next time you are angry, sad, afraid, jealous, or restless, don't try to resist the feeling, because resistance will only empower it. Instead, remind yourself that you are trying to solve a feeling that is 100% thought-created and not based in the real, external world. When you see it's a thought that is causing you to feel the way you do, you are free to let it be. You may not feel better instantly (although you might), but you'll at least stop feeding the negative feeling, acting on it, and hence making the situation worse. Furthermore, soon enough new thinking will occur to you and the world and everything in it will look different once again.

7. A Calm Mind is a Clear Mind

When faced with a problem that seems difficult, the common approach is to think or try harder. We set goals, brainstorm, analyze, and do all sorts of other things because we believe they will help us solve the problem. Our intentions are good, but our actions demonstrate a misunderstanding about how our minds work. In reality, all we are doing is adding more doing and thinking to our minds when the problem is too much thinking in the first place. The harder we try to fix it, the more our thoughts keep running around in circles at an ever-increasing pace.

It's not that the problem is inherently difficult or vexing – it only seems that way because our minds aren't clear and the only way to have a clearer mind is to reduce the amount of thinking we do. It is only with a calm, clear mind that we are able to see the problem without the distraction of our conceptual thinking.

Understanding that our thoughts create our experience at all times frees us from the drama of our emotions. It is our thinking that makes us feel sad, angry, depressed, or frustrated. It is our thinking that makes a problem appear difficult. When we recognize the role that thought plays in the creation of our experience, our mind is able to return to a calmer and, as a result, clearer state. It is only by seeing the true nature of what is happening around you and accepting it for what it is that you are able to respond accordingly. A calm mind is a clear mind.

The opposite of a calm mind is, of course, an upset mind. When the mind gets upset, it is no longer able to see what is happening clearly enough to take appropriate action. When action is born out of worry and self-doubt, it is usually superficial, inappropriate, and too late to be effective.

The more we see our thoughts as variable, the less we'll

worry about what we're thinking, the less we'll tend to our thoughts, and the less we'll think—so the better we'll perform. When we let go of the noise and clutter of our thinking, we return to our factory settings. In that state, we are all naturally calm, clear, confident, creative, resilient, and wise – without us needing to do anything about it.

What the Inside-Out Understanding Isn't

Before we wrap up this chapter, let's clarify what the inside-out understanding is and what it isn't. Although it may at first appear so, the inside-out understanding is not a set of instructions, a belief system, a religion, or a spiritual practice. Instead, it is simply a *description* of how our experience is created. That's it. It doesn't matter whether or not you believe in it or understand the inside-out nature of reality, its laws are always in effect.

The inside-out understanding is also not a formula for how to live your life. It contains no judgements nor does it compel you to behave in any particular way. You are not required to believe or practice anything, nor is there anything you can do that violates it. Just like atoms and molecules are useful in describing what matter is composed of, the inside-out understanding simply allows us to understand that what we feel at any given time isn't a function of our circumstances but rather solely the result of our thinking.

The more we see the truth of this, the more our mind naturally begins to quiet down without us having to do anything to quieten it down. No effort or practice is required. It all happens automatically because it's how our minds were designed. As our minds quieten, we return to our default state of being where what we are on the inside is in harmony with the outside world and we are able to see clearly. And when we see clearly, we find that the joy, confidence, and resilience that we are looking for have been within us all along. Regardless of our circumstances, all there is for us to do is wake up from the dream of our thinking and, as if by magic, everything else will simply fall into place.

In the next chapter, we will explore the amazing way in which our thinking creates our problems right before our eyes and how we can solve our problems before they even have a chance to arise.

"Thoughts are just ripples of the mind. When the mind is quiet, it reflects reality." –Nisargadatta Maharaj

A Quick Summary of Chapter 3

- We cannot control our external circumstances or our thoughts – the more we try, the more suffering we create for ourselves

- Whether we are aware of it or not, our experience of life is created by our thinking and not our external circumstances

- We experience life from the inside-out 100% of the time – the process only works one way and it works that way all of the time for everyone

- It's not realizing *what* we are thinking but *that* we are thinking that truly matters – people who believe everything they think tend to live in neurotic, self-created prisons

- The degree to which we understand the inside-out nature of reality largely determines our level of resilience, clarity, and wisdom in any situation

Chapter 4

The Origin of Our Problems

Last summer, some friends visited us at our summer cottage with their two beautiful daughters, aged 3 and 5. As we sat down for a meal, the girls got to choose from two plastic cups to drink from – a green one and an orange one. The younger daughter came to the table first and took the green cup. The older daughter wasn't pleased with her orange cup and got very upset. It took a long time to calm her down and get her to accept the orange cup. In her mind, not having the right colored cup was a genuine problem that caused her emotional distress.

Having to drink from the wrong colored cup probably won't cause many adults to throw a tantrum in public because we know the color of the cup doesn't really matter, but it points to the nature in which our minds create problems. So, what's the orange cup in your life? What imaginary value have you given to something that now has control over your happiness and well-being? Is it how much money you think you should have in order to feel secure, how your relationship with your spouse should be in order for you to feel loved, or how successful you need to be in order to be happy?

We all have goals we want to reach, problems we want to solve, or habits we'd like to break, and our ability to succeed with these would presumably have a significant influence on our happiness and well-being. What problem do you have that, if solved, your life would be markedly better? Perhaps it's a bad habit you'd like to kick, a goal you are yet to reach, or a relationship you'd like to improve or create. What stops you from solving your problems or achieving your goals?

It's certainly not that we don't know what to do. Although we may not like to admit it, most of us know exactly what we need to do to solve most of our problems. If we want to lose weight, we know that we need to exercise more and eat less. If we want to make more friends, we know we have to put ourselves in more social situations and overcome our shyness. Even when we don't know what to do, we can find step-by-step instructions on the internet in a matter of minutes – on virtually any topic. So clearly the problem isn't that we don't know what to do. The problem is getting ourselves to do it.

We are thus faced with one of the great human conundrums: why doesn't our desire for an outcome motivate us to take sustained action to get there? We all know the feeling of starting something and feeling full of enthusiasm and resolve to put our plan into action, only to see it fizzle out in a matter of weeks or months. And when we fail once again, our disappointment leads us to be even more judgmental of ourselves and our perceived weakness.

The questions many of us ask ourselves are: "what do I want?" or "what's my passion?" and these usually lead to rather predictable answers: most of us want a chiseled six-pack, financial success, a career as a rock star, or an erotic relationship with a supermodel. Or perhaps you want to become a zen meditator, fluent in Spanish, or learn to perform magic tricks. It's easy to want these things but wanting them doesn't get us any closer to having them.

It's quite obvious that we are asking the wrong question. Instead of asking "what do I want?", we would get better answers by asking "what am I willing to suffer for?" When we ask this question, we start from the process rather than the outcome. It's easy to want a lot of money but it's harder to serve people and make a difference in their lives. It's easy to want a chiseled six-pack but it's harder to commit to a strict diet and workout regime. The point is that if you don't like the idea of putting in the work, you probably don't *really* want the outcome (whatever it is) – you just like the *idea* of it.

The bottom line is that if you aren't willing to suffer for something and push through low motivation periods, you are unlikely to be willing to put in the work. There is nothing that you can do that is always going to be fun. It's hardly rocket science that people who generally enjoy going to the gym and maintaining a strict diet tend to be healthier and fitter. They're ok with the tradeoff, just like some people are happy to trade in their free time in order to have a family with four screaming kids and a dog. What you need to do is find something that you're happy to pay the price for. As Henry David Thoreau put it, "the price of anything is the amount of life you exchange for it."

Most of us fail without ever realizing that the cause of our failure was that we just wanted the outcome without being willing to pay the price for it. And in the post-mortem of our failure, we mistakenly identify a lack of motivation and/or will-power as the culprits. Rather than question whether our happiness *really* depends on getting "the green cup", we instead double down on our motivation and will-power. We might try to think more positively, remind ourselves of our desired outcome, or recite positive affirmations. We make detailed plans, make use of all sorts of tools and gadgets to make the work easier, and use carrots and sticks to deter ourselves from giving up yet again. Despite all that, we fail more often than not.

What is important to understand is that these failures say nothing about us or our abilities, but rather about our understanding of the core problem. The problem isn't one of motivation or will-power, but rather the result of a misunderstanding about where our experience comes from. The solution isn't found by trying to increase our motivation, will-power, or the effectiveness of our strategies – it's found by understanding the origin of the problem.

To begin this exploration, let us try to answer the most basic question: what is a problem? The dictionary defines a problem as "a matter or situation that is regarded as unwelcome and harmful and needing to be dealt with and overcome". In other words, a problem is the difference between how things are and how we think they should be. What this means is that whatever problem we are dealing with is only as big or small as what we've created in our own minds. Every problem is rooted in emotion, and the intensity of that emotion is determined by the size of the gap between what is and how we think things should be.

However, because problems are ultimately something we've created in our minds, we need to be mindful of how to go about solving them. Like the orange cup, what we generally consider to be our problems are actually symptoms. But symptoms of what?

The Source of Our Problems

Since problems are the difference between what is and what we believe should be, one solution is to find a way to bridge the gap between the two. In other words, to transform our circumstances so that they are as we expect or desire that they should be. The problem with this solution is that we need to change the external world in order to satisfy an internal preference, and the external world simply isn't under our control. No matter how much effort we put into trying to control things around us, neither the world nor our feelings will bend to our whims.

The more we wish for things to be different, the more we are likely to feel anxious, depressed, angry, or afraid. Operating from a fear-based mindset means that instead of working toward a goal from a place of balance and joy, we find ourselves trying to escape our current predicament, often from a place of fear, desperation, and urgency. Trying to escape a situation or feeling, makes staying focused on and committed to a goal incredibly challenging simply because our core objective isn't to get to a particular place, but rather to escape the place we currently find ourselves. Escaping rather than striving toward a specific, defined outcome usually means that as soon as we find ourselves even slightly away from our undesired situation or feeling, we no longer feel the need or motivation to continue, and once again, we feel that we have failed to solve the problem or make any life-changing/significant improvement.

Fortunately, accepting that we do not have control of the outside world does not mean that we shouldn't have goals, that we should be complacent about failure, or that we can settle for pain and mediocrity. Accepting that we do not have control means that we accept the way things are and therefore align ourselves with reality as opposed to how we think things should be. Once we accept our lack of control, it becomes much easier to understand that the source of our problems lies solely in our minds.

When we trace any problem back to its source, we inevitably find that the problem originates from a negative or uncomfortable feeling. In other words, it's only a problem because it makes us feel a certain way which we don't like. That feeling can range from the subtle and seemingly harmless, such as boredom or restlessness, to the intense and potentially harmful, such as anxiety, anger, or depression. Often, we are not even aware of our feelings, yet they still compel us to act because we are so conditioned to avoid uncomfortable feelings that we react to them subconsciously. It is when we act upon uncomfortable feelings that we set off a chain reaction that ends up creating most of our problems.

Fight or Flight

When we experience an uncomfortable feeling, our typical first instinct is to try to push the feeling away. This is generally accomplished through some form of distraction, such as checking social media or the news, going for a smoke, turning on the TV, or even reorganizing the linen closet.

Perhaps you noticed that the above list of common distractions reads like a list of common bad habits. This isn't a coincidence. At its core, every bad habit is a distraction we use to take our minds off an uncomfortable feeling. It only became a habit because it worked and we kept going back to it for the relief it provided. Thus, every bad habit is merely an unconscious decision to choose a distraction over having to deal with an uncomfortable feeling.

Sometimes, the uncomfortable feeling is so strong that our distraction technique doesn't work in taking our mind off it and the feelings of discomfort persist. In this situation, we typically resort to our secondary strategy, which is to look around at our circumstances for the likely cause of our suffering so that we can fix it. We interpret the uncomfortable feeling as a sign that something must be broken and that we need to fix it in order to stop feeling this way. This approach leads our minds to create a problem for us to fix, such as the need to lose weight, make more money, find a girlfriend, or be more positive.

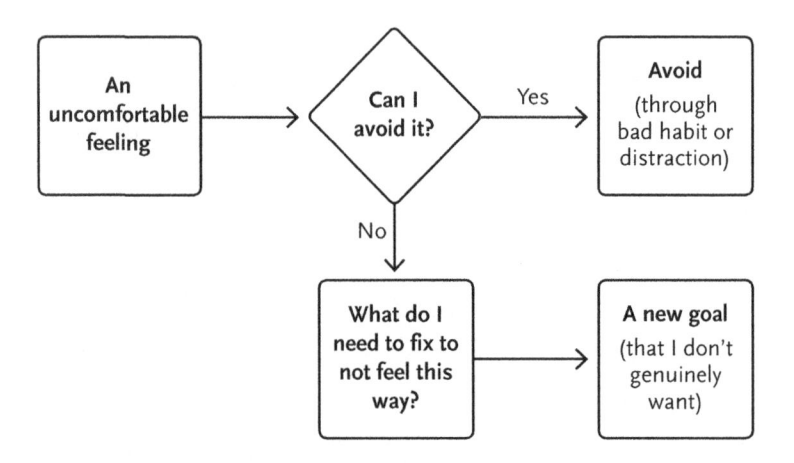

```
┌──────────────┐     ╱╲         ┌──────────────┐
│     An       │    ╱  ╲   Yes  │    Avoid     │
│ uncomfortable│──▶╱Can I╲─────▶│  (through    │
│   feeling    │   ╲avoid╱      │  bad habit or│
│              │    ╲ it?╱      │  distraction)│
└──────────────┘     ╲╱         └──────────────┘
                      │
                      │ No
                      ▼
              ┌──────────────┐  ┌──────────────┐
              │  What do I   │  │  A new goal  │
              │ need to fix to│─▶│ (that I don't│
              │ not feel this│  │   genuinely  │
              │    way?      │  │    want)     │
              └──────────────┘  └──────────────┘
```

PICTURE 11 - We try to solve our uncomfortable feelings by distracting ourselves and if that doesn't work, we find something to fix in our circumstances to alleviate our suffering.

Although our goals seem valuable in that they will improve our lives and give us a sense of happiness and achievement, we fail to comprehend that fixing an outside problem (money, relationships, winning a championship, etc) won't actually fix our inner suffering, because our inner suffering is caused by something different altogether (thought that manifests itself as an uncomfortable feeling). Thus, any goal we set to escape an uncomfortable feeling only serves as a temporary distraction from that feeling rather than a goal we truly want to achieve.

Even when we manage to succeed at whatever goal we set for ourselves, it's only a matter of time before we find ourselves again in the throes of the same feeling of boredom, loneliness, emptiness, insecurity, or worthlessness that we tried so hard to escape. In other words, solving our problems doesn't necessarily solve our problems.

The Problem with the Problem

The problem with trying to solve our problems is that what we consider to be our problems are in fact just symptoms. By focusing on the symptoms, we ignore what is really causing them in the first place. And time spent focusing on the symptoms is time not spent solving the real cause, leading us down a vicious cycle of needing bigger distractions and more audacious goals to keep the symptoms from reappearing.

For instance, many people use money as a measure of security and self-worth. Their initial goal may be to have $10,000 in the bank in order to feel financially secure but as soon as they reach this goal, they start to feel that $10,000 isn't enough, that it needs to be $50,000 or $100,000. It's easy to assume that some amount of money will finally be enough, but in most cases, it isn't. There are people who have millions of dollars who still feel financially insecure.

The misunderstanding here is trying to solve a problem with money even though lack of money is not the actual problem. The real problem is feeling insecure and then trying to pacify the insecurity with an external remedy. Thus, no matter how much money we throw at the problem, it can never be the solution. Since feelings are the result of our thinking and not our circumstances, it is futile to try to solve a feeling by rearranging our circumstances.

Whenever we start relying on a habit to feel a certain way – for instance, going for a cigarette every time we feel bored or frustrated – it's easy to become increasingly more dependent on it. One cigarette per day quickly turns into two, three, five, ten or even twenty cigarettes, and we find that when it isn't possible to go for a smoke when we want to, we feel we cannot function as well or that we're missing out. By mistaking the symptom (smoking) for the cause (boredom), we end up focusing our time and effort on tending to the symptoms, which only strengthens them and requires even larger countermeasures to deal with their effects. Any success we have in dealing with a symptom tends to become a new routine or action that we believe we need to do from now in order to avoid that bad feeling.

What we fail to realize is that these new routines and actions don't help us, they just become something we must do in order to feel okay, to keep on par. In other words, we now have one more thing we need to do to maintain the norm. Not only is this incredibly inefficient, it also clutters our life and makes it harder for us to see the true cause of our problems.

Problems Dressed Up as Goals

There is no question that goals can be incredibly useful in focusing our efforts or organizing a group of people to work toward a common cause. Unfortunately, goals are often misused and misunderstood. Perhaps the most common misuse of goals is seeing them as a means of escaping our current predicament. When we set goals with the expectation that achieving them will allow us to escape our suffering and bring about the happiness or security that we lack, we are confusing solving problems with achieving goals.

At first glance, these may not seem mutually exclusive. Fixing our insecure financial situation can be both a goal as well as a situation we desperately want to escape. What sets them apart, however, is the state of mind from which we frame the goal. From a fearful, anxious, or insecure state of mind, a goal is an escape route from our current predicament. From a secure, peaceful state of mind, a goal is a direction that we want to move toward from a place of curiosity even though we are okay where we are right now.

As such, any goal can be either a genuine *goal* (a direction we want to move in) or a *problem disguised as a goal* (a way to escape our current suffering or discomfort) depending on the state of mind in which it was created. Genuine goals are something that we work towards knowing that it's not the end of our world if we don't achieve them. Our happiness and emotional wellbeing are not at stake.

On the other hand, goals that are set in a low state of mind are actually just problems disguised as goals where our happiness seems to depend on achieving our desired outcome. Unsurprisingly, this causes us to place tremendous pressure on ourselves to succeed. This is why so many people today suffer from burnout – they have associated reaching a goal with happiness, which is why they chase their goals with everything they've got, no matter what the cost. In the process, they often end up sacrificing their relationships and health, not to mention their ability to actually enjoy the ride.

When we chase problems dressed up as goals, our motivation only lasts as long as we're feeling the effects of our problem. As soon as we get some distance from the present situation that we are trying to escape, there isn't as much motivation to keep pushing us forward. If becoming a millionaire was your goal but you set that goal because you really hated being broke, your motivation to keep working towards your goal is likely to start dwindling the moment you have enough money to not feel broke. Note that it's not the exact amount of money that is going to make or break our motivation, but how we feel about that amount in any given moment. The key determinant is our state of mind, because it can make $100 seem like plenty and $1,000,000 like not nearly enough. To further illustrate how we mistake problems for goals, consider the following example:

> Imagine you are standing bare-footed on hot coals. Your feet are burning and you are suffering greatly when you notice a snowy mountain in front of you. Ah, snow! It would feel *so* good to be standing in the cold, soothing snow. So you decide to make it your goal to climb to the top of the mountain. It seems like something you really want to do, and as soon as you start climbing the mountain, the snow begins to cool and soothe your burning feet. You feel good about your goal and the progress you are making. Soon, however, you notice that the less your feet burn, the less motivation you have to keep climbing the mountain. As the pain in your feet disappears completely, so does your motivation. You try to push yourself to keep going but find yourself resisting with each step you take. Soon you find yourself giving up, disappointed in your ability to stay disciplined and motivated enough to reach your goal.

When our core motivation for a goal is to escape our current predicament, it doesn't matter what direction we go in as long as it's away from where we are. However, as soon as we have some distance between us and what we wanted to escape from, there is nothing left to keep us going. This creates an emotional pendulum effect where we alternate between the extremes of massive effort and commitment, and total relapse and avoidance. We feel discomfort that we want to escape, so we set ambitious goals and take massive action. But as soon as our suffering starts to ease, our motivation to keep going begins to wane and we start slipping back to where we started. And soon the cycle begins anew.

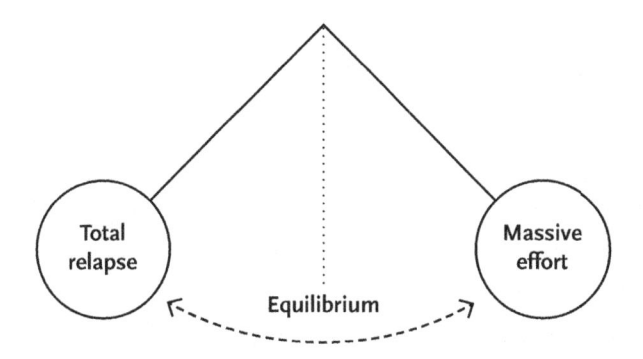

PICTURE 12 - Our emotional imbalance and desperation creates the pendulum effect where we end up alternating between the extremes of massive effort and relapse.

When we mistake our happiness as being dependent on reaching our goals, we essentially turn our goals into our personal list of reasons why we cannot be happy right now. When our happiness appears to be dependent on the achievement of a particular outcome, we become more likely to engage in destructive behavior such as taking shortcuts, neglecting our relationships, and taking advantage of others.

The more we feel that our happiness is at stake, the more it seems that the end justifies the means. We are less likely to enjoy what we do, and sometimes we even risk our own health and wellbeing to get what we want. Goals are thus useful tools when used correctly (to guide our action), but they make terrible masters when we make our emotional wellbeing dependent upon their successful completion.

Avoiding Our Feelings

Problems and bad habits are ultimately the result of our attempt to escape our uncomfortable feelings. Whether it's something as innocent as boredom or restlessness, or something a bit more intense like loneliness or feeling unloved or worthless, our desire to avoid uncomfortable feelings creates far more problems than it solves. From an early age, we've learned to react to emotional discomfort with incredible speed and efficiency to the point that we often react without requiring conscious thought to do so. This is what makes bad habits so hard to overcome. What may have started out as simply a way to distract ourselves from emotional discomfort evolved into an automatic, subconscious response to that emotion.

Most of us don't even realize what it is that prompts us to reach for our smartphone, to crave chocolate, or decide to go for a cigarette break. And when we aren't aware of what triggers our bad habit, we struggle to identify what purpose our it serves for us. Without this missing link, trying to fix bad habits tends to be a frustrating struggle because it simply relies on replacing one behavior with another, with no consideration for what purpose the bad habit served. At the end of the day, that purpose is always to distract us from some form of emotional discomfort. Until we are able to see that it is our desire to avoid emotional discomfort that underpins every bad habit, we will struggle to let go of them.

Another problem with avoiding particular feelings and experiences is that the stronger and scarier they become, the more avoiding them turns into a full-time job. For instance, if you don't feel comfortable being the center of attention (speaking up in meetings, having people celebrate your accomplishments, etc) and you decide that it's an experience you want to avoid, you are going to have to keep avoiding it for the rest of your life. You will always have to be somewhat vigilant to try to control the external circumstances around you so that you won't be put in that situation. How exhausting!

The simple reason we keep on doing this is because of the persistent illusion in life that if we are able to try just a little bit harder and a little bit longer, we will be able to control all the things that matter. Happiness and control always seem just out of reach; a few more steps, a couple more tries, or a tiny bit more effort. But the real issue isn't that we aren't trying hard enough, it's that we are running away from our experiences. This causes us to operate from a state of emotional imbalance, which leads us to adopt bad habits and pursue false goals.

Fortunately, there's another, much better option; find the source of the problem and solve it at its origin.

The Power of Surrender

What do you suppose would happen if you had an uncomfortable feeling and instead of pushing it away or trying to fix it, you did absolutely nothing? Yes, absolutely nothing. Just allowed the feeling to wash over you. Without resistance. Simply letting it happen, until the feeling passes or you become so used to it that there is no longer anything to change or fix.

Perhaps at this point you are thinking: *"Wait just a damn minute! If I feel lonely, bored, or worried and do nothing about it, how is THAT going to help solve ANYTHING?"*

At first glance, the idea of doing nothing when experiencing emotional discomfort sounds crazy. We're so conditioned to react to the slightest distress signal that the notion of relaxing into our discomfort makes about as much sense as putting your feet up and watching another episode of Modern Family when your house is on fire. Our misunderstanding is that the feelings of boredom, loneliness, worthlessness, fear, anger, rejection, and humiliation are bad feelings that we should always seek to avoid. What we fail to realize is that uncomfortable feelings are only uncomfortable because we've always pushed them away the moment we start to experience them. We mistook them for warning signs that something was wrong and that a solution was required urgently. In fact, we probably don't really know those feelings very well at all because we've always been in such a rush to get rid of them.

In many ways, an uncomfortable emotion is like red wine in that most people find their first taste rather unpleasant: *"Yuk! That wasn't anything like what I was expecting. Why do people drink this shit?"* But when another opportunity to drink wine arises some weeks later, we taste it again. Still not our thing but not as bad as we remembered it. Over time, as we keep having a glass of red wine here and another one there, we start to realize that red wine is actually rather tasty.

It is only because we kept returning to red wine with curiosity and an open mind (and perhaps some peer pressure), that over time we discovered a whole world of unique tastes and flavors that had been previously unknown to us. We realized that red wine doesn't actually taste *bad*, it just tastes *different* from everything we had experienced before, and as a result, our world expanded. Red wine was no longer something to be avoided but enjoyed.

This is more or less how it works with uncomfortable feelings. When we don't seek to avoid or fix them and instead embrace and get to know them, they gradually lose their power over us. As we become more comfortable and accepting of our uncomfortable feelings, they cease to be a problem and there is nothing left for us to avoid or fix. Our newfound comfort allows us to simply let go of the bad habits we have picked up to distract ourselves from our emotional discomfort. And just as easily, we can recognize and let go of all the superficial and inauthentic goals that we have created for ourselves out of our need to try to ease our emotional discomfort.

We all have the innate capacity to not only welcome but also enjoy negative feelings. Most people occasionally listen to sad or angry music. If sadness and anger are bad feelings, why would anyone want to listen to music that originates from those feelings? The reason is that when we are sad, there's nothing better than listening to a sad song and diving even deeper into the sadness. It just feels really good. It's like being embraced by a friend who understands our pain. Regardless of whether we feel sad, lonely, scared, angry, or heartbroken, music is a way of embracing and exploring that feeling in a deeper, non-intellectual way. Music is a way of inviting the feeling to enter us deeply and wash over us. And at some point, after we've listened to enough songs, the feeling starts to subside. We didn't overcome the feeling. We simply surrendered to it and it left us only when it was ready to go.

Getting Comfortable Being Uncomfortable

As we begin to see that uncomfortable feelings aren't a warning sign for us to flee or fix something, we learn to embrace them with a gentle curiosity. The more curious of our feelings we become, the less we run away from our experiences and the more we settle down into the center of our being. As we relax with our feelings and allow them to wash over us, our emotions stop controlling us like puppets on a string. Our problems dissolve without us having to take action, we become free to let go of our bad habits, and we gain the clarity to distinguish between goals and problems masked as goals.

Sometimes instead of accepting or welcoming our uncomfortable feelings, we unwittingly try to put up with them until the discomfort passes. When we do this, we resist the uncomfortable feelings instead of embracing them. What we are subconsciously communicating to ourselves in that moment is that we don't want this moment to be as it is, that we want to be somewhere or someone else. But resisting only intensifies our discomfort, irritates us, and tires us out. Surrendering to an uncomfortable feeling isn't an exercise of strength and willpower, but one of patience and gentleness. Our objective is not to defiantly outlast our pain, but to surrender to it, to embrace it, to be a little bit gentler with it and ourselves than we were before. That uncomfortable feeling is our guest, not a threat or an enemy needing to be dealt with.

When we approach whatever uncomfortable feeling we have from this perspective, there is nothing to fix, nothing to distract ourselves from, and nothing to push away. All that is required is to simply be, and allow the feeling to be, with a sense of gentle curiosity. Don't listen to any story your mind might try to tell you to justify the feeling. Ignore the story and instead just feel the feeling as fully as you can.

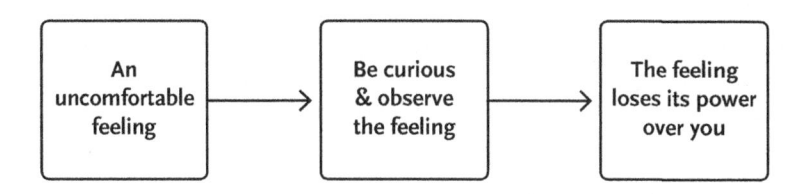

An uncomfortable feeling → Be curious & observe the feeling → The feeling loses its power over you

PICTURE 13 - The paradox of surrender: the "solution" to uncomfortable feelings is to not fix them, but to surrender to them until they give up their power over you.

At first when you try this, you may notice your feelings of discomfort getting more intense, but that's only because you aren't used to it. Whatever you do, don't pull away and don't close down. Stay with your discomfort with an open heart and you will soon notice the discomfort begin to subside. After a while, you will notice that the feeling doesn't actually feel that bad – it just feels different and sometimes enjoyable, sort of like a glass of red wine you once learned to enjoy. The longer you stay with the feeling, the more you will naturally accept it and the need or desire to push it away will simply disappear. Eventually, what you considered your enemy will turn into a close, trusted friend – or at the very least an amicable acquaintance. When you no longer need to resist the feeling, something unexpected happens; you are no longer feeding the uncomfortable feeling energy, and as a result, it moves on more quickly.

By cultivating an awareness to embrace our uncomfortable feelings as they arise, we develop the ability to dissolve our problems before they have the chance to manifest into something real. This saves us from adopting bad habits and committing to inauthentic goals simply to "fix" the uncomfortable feeling inside. Instead, we go straight to the source and solve it there – or perhaps more accurately, we allow the "problem" to dissolve there. This not only frees up time and energy, but it also helps us gain a tremendous sense of clarity about our lives, what we truly want, and what we need to do in any given moment.

Just imagine how powerful we would be if we didn't need to protect ourselves from negative feelings such as loneliness, disappointment, rejection, or humiliation. How much extra energy would we have if we didn't need to constantly protect ourselves from uncomfortable feelings and situations that may cause them? How much more balanced would we be if we weren't being pushed and pulled by fear and desperation? Most of all, imagine how free we would be to attempt *anything*, because our sense of happiness and wellbeing would not be tied to an external outcome or the approval of others.

It's rather amazing to realize that all our potential is right at our fingertips. More amazing still is that in order to tap into this potential, we don't need to do anything. Instead of running away from emotional discomfort or trying to tackle it head on, we can just let it be. Rather than trying to put up with the emotional discomfort, we can welcome it in and give it a place to rest and eventually dissolve. The very door we open for our emotional discomfort to enter is the same door through which it is able to exit.

> *"We're all in a free fall into future. We don't know where we're going. Things are changing so fast, and always when you're going through a long tunnel, anxiety comes along. And all you have to do to transform your hell into a paradise is to turn your fall into a voluntary act. It's a very interesting shift of perspective and that's all it is... joyful participation in the sorrows and everything changes."* – Joseph Campbell, Sukhavati

A Quick Summary of Chapter 4

- What appears to be our problem is actually a symptom of our attempt to avoid or fix our uncomfortable feelings

- Bad habits are the result of successfully and habitually avoiding our uncomfortable feelings

- When we can't avoid uncomfortable feelings, we start looking for what's causing them in our lives. But because we're looking in the wrong places, we easily end up mistaking problems for goals

- The most effective way to deal with our problems is by going to the source – our uncomfortable emotions – and (dis)solving them there

- The more comfortable we become with emotional discomfort, the less impact it has on our lives and the more we are free to pursue any goal we choose

Chapter 5

The Secret of Performance

So far in this book, we've explored two main insights:

- Our experience of reality is made up 100% of thought and that our thinking – and thus our experience of reality – is always in flux.
- Our inability to see the thought-feeling connection leads us to create our problems and bad habits, because our misunderstanding causes us to spend our energy and attention on trying to control our experience by manipulating the outside world and our own thinking.

In this chapter, we will explore the implications of the inside-out understanding on performance and what it really means to perform at your best regardless of the situation. Most of us believe that there is some piece of information or knowledge so valuable out there that if we could gain possession of it, it would instantly transform our lives. It sounds so irresistibly simple. Just find the one key piece of advice that's missing and you'll solve your problem with ease.

If this sounds familiar, it's probably because it's how thousands of "revolutionary" new diets, exercises, self-help books, and investment strategies are marketed to us. If we only knew exactly what to do, we too could get the results we desire. You have probably seen this approach in countless marketing materials: "Seven proven techniques for losing weight" or "12 easy ways to skyrocket your motivation". If we put this way of thinking into a formula, it would look something like this:

> **PERFORMANCE = POTENTIAL + INFORMATION**

PICTURE 14 - The common misunderstanding about the source of performance. Information isn't the missing ingredient.

The thinking behind this formula essentially states that we'd achieve great results if only we had the information to best fulfill our potential. Once we have the missing piece of information, all that is left is for us to practice it so we can implement it. If we did a survey about the aspects that most people would like to improve about themselves, we'd probably end up with a list something like this:

Confidence	Assertiveness
Connection	Peace
Resilience	Creativity
Love	Joy
Wisdom	Self-esteem

PICTURE 15 - Common qualities that people would like to improve about themselves.

Throughout history, mankind has developed strategies and methods to maximize each of these. But despite thousands of years of trial and error, we don't appear to have made much progress. Humans universally continue to lack confidence, resilience, peace, and joy like our great ancestors before us. Could the problem be that we haven't found the right information to unlock our potential? It seems highly unlikely that *no one* has stumbled upon the answer yet.

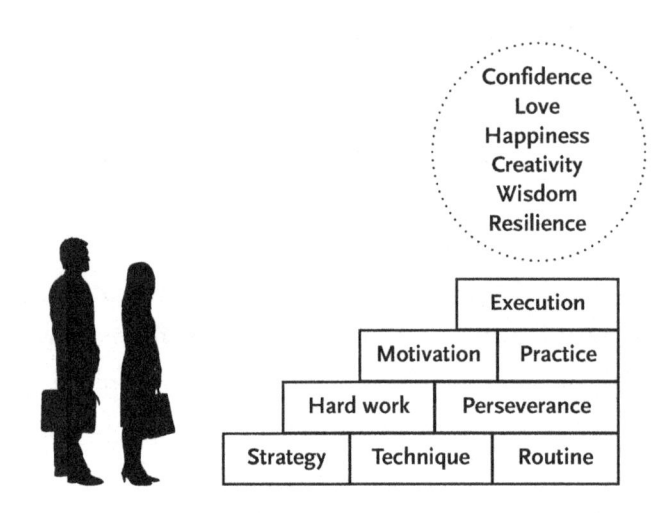

PICTURE 16 - The common view is that we need strategies, motivation and discipline in order to feel happy, confident, and resilient.

A much more likely explanation is that we've been looking in all the wrong places due to a fundamental misunderstanding about where human performance stems from. One major reason we struggle to improve our results is that we confuse what is innate and what is a skill that needs to be practiced and implemented.

Although the "missing information" theory that most of us have bought into seems logical, a simple glance at our own results shows otherwise. We are constantly taking in information and learning strategies and techniques, but how much of what we've learned and know do we actually apply? As Michael Neill points out in his remarkable book *The Space Within*, when we look closely at our results, we see that they correlate less with what we know than with what we do. Therefore, the missing ingredient is not information, but instead whatever it is that *prevents* us from taking action. If we rewrite the formula from this perspective, it would look like this:

> **PERFORMANCE = POTENTIAL − INTERFERENCE**

PICTURE 17 - Understanding that performance is innate and that our conscious thinking interferes with it is the key to performing better.

This formula was first articulated by Timothy Gallwey in his ground-breaking book *The Inner Game of Tennis*. What the formula points to is that when we eliminate interference, we perform closer to our full potential. Creativity, joy, resilience, love, confidence, and wisdom are all qualities of our default state rather than things we need to learn, practice, and implement. So how do we access these default qualities? By eliminating the interference. How do we eliminate the interference? First, we need to understand what it is and where it comes from, and I suspect you have an idea of the answer already. Our thinking.

Neuroscientists estimate that the average person has anywhere from 50,000 to 80,000 thoughts per day. The average adult also makes about 35,000 decisions per day, although many of which are made unknowingly. Thoughts are the clay from which we form our moment-to-moment experience, and it isn't difficult to see that when we get caught up in our thinking, we rather easily lose our bearings. In other words, the moment we start overthinking, we get cut off from our deeper intelligence. We find ourselves adding more thoughts to something that would be best solved by reducing our conscious thinking.

The Things That Trip Us Up

To illustrate how this works in practice, imagine that you are trying to start a new business, but you aren't exactly sure how to go about it. At first glance, the problem would seem to be lack of information. But if you look back on your life, has a lack of information *always* stopped you? Of course it hasn't. Without a doubt, there have been plenty of instances along the way when you've lacked information but a quick call to a friend or an online search provided you with the necessary information and you proceeded with your task without a second thought. Clearly, a lack of information doesn't always stop you.

However, what if you are lacking confidence to do something, like asking someone out on a date or giving a speech to a room full of people? A shortage of confidence certainly looks like a genuine barrier that is holding you back. But upon closer reflection, you will no doubt realize that a lack of confidence hasn't *always* prevented you from taking action. I'm sure you can recall several occasions in your life when you've done something even though you didn't feel confident at the time, because it's not actually a lack of confidence that is ever holding us back.

If neither external (e.g. lack of info) or internal (e.g. lack of confidence) obstacles stop us all the time, then what is it that does? Why does lack of time or self-discipline prevent us from going for a 20-minute jog one day but the next day we, despite everything being the same, we happily throw on our jogging shoes and eagerly head out the door? It's rather curious that our obstacles seem to stop us in some instances but not in others.

The reason for this is that it's not the barrier that stops us but rather the state of mind we're in when we think about the barrier. From a low mental state, obstacles seem insurmountable; everything seems difficult, uncertain, and futile. But when we're in a good mental state, barriers suddenly seem like little challenges, speed bumps, or a quick climb up a ladder to get to the next level. This is a vital distinction, because it points to the fact that however something looks – difficult or easy, simple or complicated, fun or boring – it's all in the mind of the beholder.

Being in the right mental state not only lets us view the obstacle from a more empowered perspective that enables us to see solutions that we couldn't see before, but it is also the key that unlocks our hidden potential to perform at our highest capacity. So how do we influence our mental state? Curiously, it all starts from acknowledging a familiar but grossly overlooked part of our lives – the voice in our heads.

The Voice In Your Head

Have you noticed the voice inside your head that constantly narrates your experience? From the moment you open your eyes in the morning, the voice starts talking and says things such as these:

> "Ugh, I wish I could just keep on sleeping."
> "Why does the garbage truck always come so early?!"
> "It's going to be epic to catch up with the guys tonight."
> "F*#k. The rent is due today."
> "I need coffee before I can even think about doing anything."
> "I can't believe Geoff still hasn't replied to my email!"
> "Man, I'm out of shape. I've got to start going to the gym."

These are just a few examples of thoughts we all commonly have – sometimes we can have all of these in just the first minute of being awake. And the narration continues throughout the day – it's there in almost all our waking moments.

Now, if you are reading this and thinking *"What are you talking about? I don't have a voice in my head"*, then that's *exactly* the voice I am talking about. We are so used to this constant voice in our heads that we barely realize it's there, incessantly narrating our experience. You have probably come to think of the voice as you, because it guides most of your waking moments. But that voice isn't you. *You* are the one who actually *hears* that voice. From this simple observation, we can deduce (and philosophers have for thousands of years) that we are comprised of not one but two selves.

The voice that you hear in your head is what is sometimes referred to as the "teller". The teller guides most of your waking moments and constantly narrates your experience. The second self – the real you – is the one who hears the teller. This self is known as the "doer" (or consciousness), because its job isn't to narrate and comment but rather to take action. It is the doer who takes the necessary steps to achieve your goals, however big or small, for example, getting out of bed.

Most of us have come to rely on our teller as the source of control in our lives, but it is in fact the doer that has the power to solve problems and get things done, not the teller. Since most of us are not aware of our two selves, we've unknowingly assigned all the power to our teller. The belief that we are the teller and that we are in control is a misunderstanding that causes us many problems.

When the teller is left in charge and given too much authority, it starts to interfere with the doer. Almost invariably, this leads to a deterioration in our performance, creativity, self-discipline, and inner wisdom. The reason for this is that the teller communicates in a way that disrupts the doer. The teller is constantly pushing us to "try harder", "do more", and "not make a mistake". It scolds and judges us when we don't perform up to its expectations, telling us that "we suck", "we'll never learn", and "we don't deserve it". The more the teller is in charge, the harder we try and the tenser we become. And when we get tense from trying too hard or from trying to avoid making a mistake, we block our natural responses (i.e. the doer), leading to an inevitable drop in performance. The end result of the teller's influence is that our doer-self is sabotaged and unable to execute in the natural way it knows how.

In practice, an over-bearing teller means that it becomes harder to make good decisions, perform in front of an audience, listen to our inner wisdom, be our authentic selves, play well in an important situation, have the discipline to stick with our plan, or ignore our cravings and addictions.

You might be wondering, if the teller is such a problem, why don't we just stop listening to it? Why, indeed! There are a few layers to this. First of all, we don't realize that the teller is made up 100% of thought. It isn't real. The voice that you hear is just excess mental energy, sort of like a tea pot that whistles to get rid of the excess steam. The second reason is that we don't understand that we are not the teller, so we perceive the world from the teller's limited perspective. The third reason is that we don't trust the doer to be able to do what needs to be done and as a result we try to micromanage and manipulate it. It is this lack of trust in our natural abilities that empowers the teller at the expense of the doer. All that does however, is cause stress and throw the doer out of sync.

The teller thrives on anxiety and fear. The more anxiety there is in our lives, the louder and more active our teller gets and the harder it is to allow the doer to perform its job. Trying harder, scolding ourselves, addiction to to-do lists, feeling urgency, and judging ourselves are all common signs that our teller is wielding too much power and that our doer is unable to perform properly. The teller seeks patterns and exceptions based on what it already knows, but is unable to come up with new ideas or insights.

The Link Between Mental State and Performance

Although countless mental trainers may tell you differently, there is actually nothing we can do to improve our mental performance consistently and reliably. Rituals, mindfulness exercises, and visualizations only pack more thought into our minds and ignore the fact that we are at our best when our minds are clear. The best thing we can do is get out of our own way, which allows us to act freely and make use of everything that is there for us in the moment. When our mind is clear, we automatically enjoy a higher state of mind and we perform better.

In the West, this higher mental state is often referred to as "flow", while in the East it's known by the Zen symbol *enso*, which symbolizes a moment when the mind is free to let the body create. Whatever you call it, it is the bedrock of excellent performance, creativity, and innate wisdom, and it usually only appears when our mind is not interfering with our 'doing'. In the flow state, performance comes naturally and unforced, it just flows out of us – almost as if it flows *through* us. In fact, many of the world's greatest athletes, artists, and inventors have confessed that they cannot explain where their greatest ideas, performances, and moments of inspiration came from. This is the magic that happens when the teller doesn't interfere with the doer. And it all begins with trusting our doer.

The decision to trust our doer requires that we let go of our need to control our circumstances and our thinking. It means we are willing to ride the waves and accept that, at times, life is going to be challenging and we will sometimes experience unpleasant thoughts and feelings. By accepting these ideas, we find freedom from the thoughts that try to protect us yet at the same time prevent us from growing.

The moment we realize that instead of *making* things happen, our only job is to *allow* them to happen, our lives transform. There's no need to push, force, or control. Our optimal performance is produced not through straining or grinding, but rather through relaxing and trusting the doer to find the right solution to the situation.

For most of our waking moments, our two selves divide

our experience. There's the teller who narrates, analyzes, and thinks, and there's the doer, who only experiences what is happening. In those moments where we are able to let go of the teller and allow the doer to emerge, our experience is no longer divided into two perspectives. Instead, we become one with the experience; we find that we are no longer narrating, judging, and trying to control the experience, but rather we are immersed in it with every fiber of our being. This not only allows us to react from a deeper place to what is happening around us, it also feels really good. Almost all our pain is the byproduct of thinking. Without thinking, we can just be 100% immersed in the moment, entirely in the present.

In case you are wondering whether letting go of the teller, making way for the doer, and allowing things to happen means that we just sit back, do nothing, and expect results to magically appear, the answer is no. It means that we stop obsessing about the outcome and accept that things won't always go the way we planned. And that's ok. It doesn't matter. It's life. Even when things aren't going right, we know that there's nothing we can do better by getting up in our heads. Instead, we stay in the game, because our doer is the one with the most potential to figure it out.

Most people actively try to avoid or escape difficult situations because of the stress and pressure they associate with it. They stop making cold calls, going to auditions or asking people out. Although this may seem like a perfectly logical course of action to them, in reality their reaction is counterproductive, unnecessary, and could be avoided if it weren't for a fundamental misunderstanding about the source of their experience. More specifically, they are confusing their emotional investment in the outcome with taking action.

Most of us are culturally conditioned to believe that a certain level of stress, pressure, or desperation is required for us to be and perform at our best. But when we examine our own lives a little closer, we see that we usually perform best when we aren't overly concerned with the outcome and we throw ourselves fully into whatever it is we are doing.

The more emotionally invested we are in something, the more we tend to obsess and stress over the end result. Rather than simply taking action, we spend our resources ourselves trying to manipulate others and our circumstances to ensure we get what we want rather than simply taking action. In order to avoid uncomfortable feelings such as failure, frustration, or anxiety, many of us tend to reduce our investment in the process to protect ourselves. But rather than reducing our *emotional investment* in the outcome, we tend to pull back completely and stop taking action.

It isn't difficult to see that when we stop taking action in order to protect ourselves from negative experiences, we aren't going to make much progress or accomplish great things. In our desire to protect ourselves from pain (i.e. negative feelings), we've mistaken the outcome and the outside world for causing our feelings, when it is in fact our high emotional investment in the outcome that is the true source of our suffering.

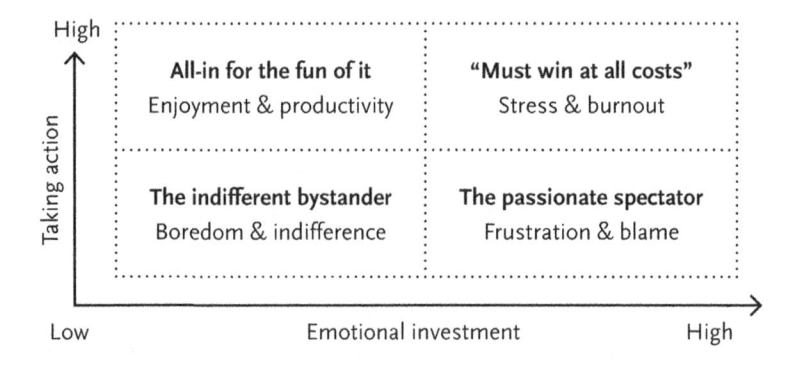

High ↑ Taking action	**All-in for the fun of it** Enjoyment & productivity	**"Must win at all costs"** Stress & burnout
	The indifferent bystander Boredom & indifference	**The passionate spectator** Frustration & blame
	Low — Emotional investment — High	

PICTURE 18 - The relationship between emotional investment and taking action is a key determinant in how we behave and perform.

Meanwhile, a low emotional investment means we don't worry about the outcome, how we are doing, or how we might look. Our focus remains solely on the job at hand, putting one foot in front of the other, and trusting that the end result will take care of itself. Many people feel justified in worrying about the outcome, constantly measuring their progress and trying to predict what the end result will be, but this only hurts their chances because they are diverting their energy and focus away from what they're doing. One of the biggest reasons so many of us fail to grow and make an impact in the world is because we are wasting so much of our energy resisting ourselves by doubting, fearing, analyzing, and second-guessing.

I truly believe the average person wastes at least half of their energy (sometimes almost all of it) resisting themselves rather than taking on whatever challenge they might be faced with. The cause of this is simple: a high emotional investment in the outcome creates emotional blockages, which usually manifest themselves in the form of stress, depression, and inner resistance. As a result, we procrastinate, over-plan and don't jump all in with both feet to our endeavors. Fortunately, all we need to do – or indeed *can* do – is wake up to the fact that the teller and the emotional investment in the outcome are simply made up of thought; they're not real, although at times it feels like they are.

If an empty mind is key to performing at our best, how do we explain athletes and other performers who visibly psyche themselves up using positive self-talk and perform at championship level? There's no question that positive thinking and motivational self-talk can help us get into a better mental state, but it makes us dependent on always being able to be positive. This is problematic because, as we all know, we can't always be positive. What do we do when we are feeling negative or insecure? Do we skip playing the game, attending the meeting, or pitching the business idea until we feel better? Obviously not.

Fortunately, when it comes to performance, it doesn't matter what mental state we are in. Sure, it's great if we're in a confident, pumped up state of mind, but even when we are feeling insecure, anxious, or afraid before an important event, it doesn't matter as long as we avoid coping techniques and mental tools. The problem with coping techniques is that we ultimately cannot rely on being able to consciously change our mental state when we need to. Often, our attempts to fix our mental state only results in even more thinking and interference, thereby actually making our mental state worse.

Since the problem is too much thinking, anything that

adds more thinking is not going to help us. It's only going to add to the mental clutter. As counter-intuitive as that sounds, it is only when we leave our mind alone that it can naturally and effortlessly self-correct to a higher mental state where we will experience clarity and confidence once again. Most people see this and think they need to meditate or do mindfulness exercises. But in the short term, even those techniques add thinking before they help dispel it. This points to the fact that the answer cannot be found in doing, practicing or thinking our way out of our funk. What we need then is a way to calm our mind down without adding thinking.

The best way to do that is simply by seeing that we will be ok regardless of whether or not we make the game-winning kick or the big sale. It is only by knowing that we will be 100% ok whatever the outcome that we can effortlessly let go of our emotional investment and allow our mind to reset itself. This allows our innate curiosity, creativity and playfulness to shine through.

This implies that we can take action even when we are not in an optimal mental state, because our mental state is always changing and sooner or later it *will* automatically self-correct. Our mental state is only an obstacle when we believe that it is. When we try to cope with our troubled mental state, we only interfere with the self-correcting mechanism and we risk obstructing our inbuilt psychological immune system.

To illustrate this in practice, consider fire fighters. Fire fighters – just like the rest of us – occasionally feel tired, insecure, and anxious. The only difference is that the moment the alarm goes off and it's time to jump into the fire truck and head toward a burning building, it no longer matters how they are feeling. Fire fighters intrinsically know that their mental state is not important for them to do their jobs and that their minds will automatically self-correct when they simply get on with their work. The reason this truth is obvious to a fire fighter but not necessarily to artists, athletes, or business people is that a fire fighters' work is sudden and immediate. There's an alarm and you just have to go. In most other professions, we have time to think and ruminate about what may or may not happen in the coming hours or days. In other words, the reason that so many of us allow our mental state to trip us up is because we have too much thinking about it. If we simply ignored our mental state and got on with what needs to be done, our minds would automatically self-correct and what seemed like a massive problem just moments ago would simply dissolve into thin air.

What this points to is that even though we may not feel confident in the moment, we can still be confident in our natural abilities (i.e. our doer and its ability to step up) at all times. In other words, we cannot always think confidently, but we *can* be confident regardless of what we are thinking. As humans, our minds are always fluctuating between clutter and clarity, but what's important to realize is that neither one affects our ability to excel – unless we let it. If we are waiting, expecting or trying to make our mind clear again before we believe we can perform at our best, we are only going to prolong our low mental state. Our full potential is always there within us. All we need to do is get out of the way and stay in the game. Our psychological immune system will take care of the rest.

If an empty mind is the conduit to performance, what can we do to stop thinking? The answer is... nothing. Even trying not to think is too much, because trying not to think just adds more thought. Instead, it is understanding why we are overthinking – because human beings are thinkers – that slows down our thinking. Whenever we look outside (i.e. the world, our circumstances, other people, ourselves, our behavior, looks, health, brain, belief system, values, aspirations, character, personality, etc.) to explain our overthinking mind, our thinking just gets louder. The reason for this is that when we look for answers outside where they cannot be found, we will only create more confusion. But when we look inside (i.e. the source of our experience – our thinking), our thinking seems to quiet down. To put it another way, if performance, creativity, and peace are derived from a state of no thought, it makes little sense to seek them by filling the mind with even more thought.

Thus, the key to performance is noticing that we are thinking, not what we are thinking about.

Noticing thoughts of *any* kind – negative, positive, even blissful thoughts – can often take us from our state of connection and flow. If you're wondering how noticing good thoughts can lead you into trouble, it's because as soon as we have thinking about our thinking, we are adding more thinking to our minds and can therefore not be as connected to the world around us.

To illustrate this in practice, here's something you can experiment with. On a day that you are playing or performing really well, simply ask yourself what you might be doing or have done differently today compared to usual. The moment you redirect your focus from what flows naturally from within to potential causes on the outside, your mental state will begin to shift from clarity to clutter, and your performance is likely to suffer. When we seek answers from outside, we are bringing in more thinking. When we look inside, we find our own answers and our performance simply flows out of us.

When we are fully immersed in what we are doing (i.e. "in the zone" or "in the state of flow"), we don't notice any thoughts – not even positive ones – in our heads. That's because getting caught up in a thought, whether negative or positive, begins to disengage us from our natural flow and take us out of our zone. In the zone, we are not divided into two selves, instead we experience everything directly as one being. We perform at our optimal level when our thinking isn't interfering with our doing.

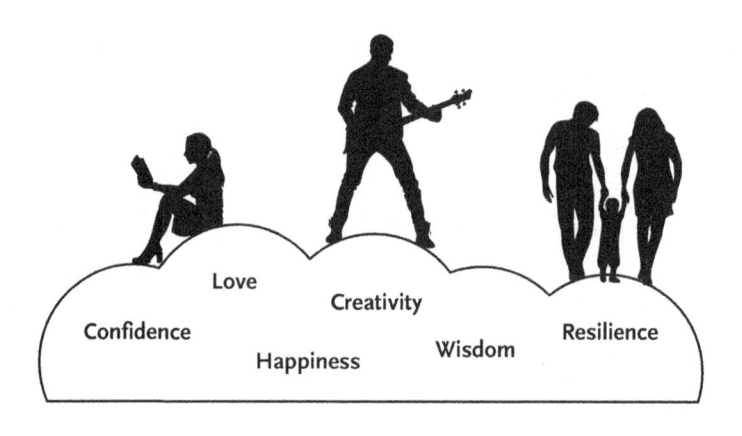

PICTURE 19 - Confidence, resilience, joy, and wisdom are our default state. There's nothing we need to do to attain them. We are them.

And that's where we find the secret of our performance – within ourselves, without us having to do anything about it. Confidence, clarity, wisdom, and resilience are our default nature. The more we see the truth of that, the less likely we are to use mental tools or coping strategies that interfere with and disrupt our self-correcting psychological immune system. Just like the sun is always there even when clouds may prevent us from seeing it, confidence, resilience, and wisdom are always there. All that is required of us is to look inside, to realize that the only thing that stands between us and our true potential is our own thinking – sort of like the sun is always there even though sometimes clouds block our view of it. And when we look within, without having to do any of the heavy lifting, everything will simply fall into place.

A Quick Summary of Chapter 5

- Contrary to popular belief, the missing ingredient of better performance is not more or better information, but rather the elimination of interference

- That interference is the result of the outside-in misunderstanding in general and, in particular, the use of coping strategies and mental tools in particular

- Our state of mind is what makes an obstacle look like an insurmountable mountain or a small speed bump in the road

- Our teller's job is to set a goal and communicate it to the doer, but it often feeds on our anxieties and insecurities and takes control of the entire enterprise

- Our doer has access to all our subconscious potential, but is easily disrupted by an over-active, micromanaging teller

- High emotional investment usually leads to either pulling back from action or stress, burnout, and an emotional rollercoaster

- A low emotional investment combined with taking action is the foundation from which effortless success springs forth

- However we might be feeling is irrelevant to our ability to excel

Chapter 6

Living from the Inside-Out

As we begin the final chapter of this book, let's take stock of what we've explored so far. We already know that:

- Our experience of reality is a unique and constantly changing mental creation,
- Our problems are all self-created illusions,
- The key to performance is simply getting on with it regardless how we might be feeling, and
- The only place to find answers is within.
- But now that we know all this, what do we do with this information? What are the next steps?

After learning about the inside-out nature of reality, most people experience feelings of peace, well-being, and clarity more often and more intensely. We can't shake the habit that action is required to achieve these feelings again. However, these moments are often just that; fleeting moments, that disappear as quickly as they came and can leave us wanting more. And so the search for more clarity continues, even though deep down we know that the act of searching is not the way to get there.

Many of us have been searching for salvation, pleasure, and success for so long that we have become addicted to the thrill of seeking. Rather than trusting and following our inner wisdom, we feel the need to intellectually understand the inside-out experience better. We struggle to shake the idea that action is required to find these moments again. But rather than create higher levels of clarity, presence, and peace for ourselves, our seeking tends to result in an endless loop of consuming ever more knowledge. In our effort to grasp this simple concept, we have turned it into an intellectual game of hide and seek.

While there is nothing wrong with trying to gain a deeper understanding of the inside-out nature of life, doing so by only reading about the experiences and insights of others is backwards. We already have the answers inside us. Searching for them elsewhere only takes us further from them. Furthermore, sitting on the sideline trying to figure things out isn't where the magic is – it's out there in the real world and the only way to access it is by getting on with our lives. Only by immersing ourselves in life, can we find the life-changing understanding that we seek.

This, then, is the purpose of this chapter; to explore what *living* from the inside-out means so that you can get on with living and enjoying your life. Put another way, giving you a theoretical or intellectual understanding of the inside-out nature of experience is about as useful as giving you an intellectual understanding of how to balance yourself on a bicycle. Before you get on the bike and start pedaling, all the advice in the world is useless. In fact, the more we read and study various concepts and teachings, the more likely we are to become extremely intelligent idiots, because our heads fill up with more and more thinking and we have less space to be present and hear our deeper wisdom.

So rather than fill your head with intellectual concepts, ideas, teachings, and frameworks, the aim of this chapter is to give you an embodied understanding of this topic. When you are finished with this book, it is my hope that you will have a practical, gut-level understanding of how your mind works and how to align yourself with it, and by default, with life itself. If we are to succeed, you will not have to think about the inside-out nature of experience as you live your daily life any more than you need to think about how to balance yourself on a bicycle. You will simply understand that everything emanates from your mind. You will *feel* it, and you can simply get on with your life.

So where do we begin? A logical point to begin this exploration is by examining the nature of our experience more closely. The dichotomy of the inside-out understanding is that our experience is simultaneously illusory and the only thing we will ever have. If we simply left it at "thought creates feeling", we would miss out on the incredible depth and wisdom that our feelings contain, and it is exactly this wisdom that holds the key to living life from the inside-out.

Understanding the thought-feeling connection is what allows us to explore the nature of our experience in more detail. On one hand, thoughts are nothing more than the paintbrush with which we create our experience from moment to moment. On the other hand, thoughts are the single most powerful creative force in the world – they can make one moment feel like heaven and the next one like hell. They have the power to heal or destroy, unify or divide. It is in this juxtaposition that the true power of thought lies; it is trivial and daunting all at once. And even though we know that our experience is completely created by thought, experience is ultimately all that we have. There really is nothing else. And just because our thoughts are illusions, doesn't mean that the experiences they create are trivial.

What this points to is that even though we know that it's all made up, there's no reason not to enjoy the roller coaster ride of feelings that make us human. There can be no highs without lows. When we understand that all experiences are equal, we can simply go along for the ride and marvel at the range of experiences the paintbrush of our mind creates from the same circumstances.

What gets us in trouble is when we interfere with our experience by trying to avoid or fix unwanted feelings, or when we try to hold onto good ones. Rather than understanding that our experience isn't the result of the outside world, we try to control our circumstances, manipulate our mental states, and avoid things that we *believe* will make us feel uncomfortable. Despite our best intentions, all this does is pack more thought on top of thought and our minds become more cluttered and opaque.

Once we see that thought is just spiritual energy and that we are not actually the thinker but rather the receiver of that energy, our experience of life transforms. We begin to understand that although it sometimes really looks like our circumstances are creating our feelings, what we are really feeling is the fluctuation of our spiritual energy (i.e. thought) and that it will inevitably change regardless of our circumstances. This means that there's nothing we can do that can make us happy all the time. Nothing will put a permanent smile on our face. The only thing that is certain is that there will be moments of happiness and moments of sadness, moments of fear and moments of comfort, moments of insecurity and moments of peace – regardless of what we have, who we are with, and where we are.

To put it in other words, happiness is *random*. It comes and it goes, just like our mind ebbs and flows. Feeling sad, anxious, or afraid doesn't mean that something is wrong – it's simply a reminder for us to take our thinking less seriously. That's all. There's nothing to change or fix. When we see the truth of this deeply enough, it opens up a totally new way of experiencing and being in the world.

When we see that happiness – like all other emotions – is random and out of our control, it loses its place as the centerpiece of our lives. This sets us free to explore and experience life in a completely different way. We no longer need guarantees how things will work out before we start them, nor do we need to know whether doing something will make us happy or not.

Without happiness (or any other emotion) to attain or arrive at, we become free to follow our curiosity and wisdom in the moment. We can try things we might not like, hang out with people we wouldn't normally hang out with, and visit places we would normally avoid. We can speak our mind and be labelled stupid. We can offer our ideas and be rejected. We can tell someone how we feel and have them not reciprocate the feeling. The point is that none of it matters when we realize that the outside world is not the source of our experiences. There's nothing we can do that will make us feel happy, secure, accepted, or loved. It's entirely an inside job. We are simply here to experience and enjoy the show. All of it.

Even though it's all so deceptively simple, many people still struggle to let go of the chase for happiness because they worry that it will make them complacent and lazy. They believe that fear, pressure, and desperation are necessary to keep them working and striving to improve their lives and circumstances. What they fail to see is that working from a place of emotional desperation leads us to pursue problems dressed up as goals rather than real goals themselves. By chasing pleasure and salvation, we are essentially trying to quench our thirst by drinking salt water. We do not realize that every extreme exists only in relation to the other: pleasure exists only in relation to pain, just like mountains exist only in relation to valleys. To try and separate the two is impossible.

The problem with emotional desperation is that it is rooted in fear, and fear causes our minds to contract in the same way that we physically contract as we brace for impact. In the contracted state, we are expending a lot of energy simply trying to hold everything in place. We do not have the freedom to react freely, to see all the options that may be available to us, because fear puts blinders on our eyes and prevents us from seeing the totality of our situation. This means that although fear may cause us to try harder, it generally requires a high expenditure of energy that isn't sustainable in the long term and causes us to approach our situation from an unclear state of mind.

The irony is that when we understand that our experience is created from within, it not only tends to help us relax and enjoy life more, but we also tend to enjoy our work more, do it more creatively and passionately, and, as a result, achieve better results. When there is nothing to fear, there is no reason to hold back, be lazy or procrastinate. Without fear, we are free to attempt anything we want, because neither failure nor criticism have any control over how we feel.

When we realize that there really is no connection between our circumstances and our feelings, it becomes evident that there is nothing we can do to make ourselves feel better. However we are feeling is the result of the ebb and flow of our spiritual energy (thinking). When we see the truth of this, it becomes apparent that what has gotten us in trouble all this time is trying to control things that are beyond our control: how other people behave, what happens in the world around us, and what we think and feel. Because all these things are outside our control, there really is no other option other than to accept them as they are and not waste time or effort on trying to control something that already is. This doesn't mean that we become apathetic, but accepting how something is and not getting worked up about it frees up our minds to notice the beauty in the little things, to have insights that would have previously been missed, and to see alternative ways of doing things. In other words, when we stop trying to fix and control how we feel, our minds have the chance to settle, and we put ourselves in a much better place to deal with whatever is in front of us.

Hearing Our Deeper Wisdom

Much of the stress and struggle we experience in life isn't because we don't know what to do, but rather the consequence of believing that we are supposed to be able to figure everything out with the intelligence of our conscious mind. In the grand scheme of things, the information we have and what we have experienced in life is but a drop in the ocean. Add a cluttered mind and it's easy to see how limited our conscious thinking really is. Even our imagination (from the perspective of when we are consciously trying to imagine something) is incredibly limited because it is confined to the ideas and concepts that we already know. Fortunately, we all have access to fresh, new thoughts and insights that we've never had before. By emptying our minds, i.e. freeing it of thinking about controlling things that cannot be controlled, our mind naturally settles and finds the space and freedom to be open and receptive to completely new thinking.

As we begin to see that we don't need to know and control everything and that we can in fact rely on a deeper sense of wisdom, it no longer makes as much sense to force an answer or operate under extreme levels of self-created pressure. Our minds work better when we don't try to intellectually do too much. To illustrate the limits of our conscious mind, behavioral scientists have shown that we can only hold 5 to 9 things in our conscious mind at once. Our subconscious mind, however, has the ability to make infinitely more connections than that. In fact, neuroscientists have found that our subconsciousness manages 90% of everything we do regardless whether we're awake or asleep. The point is that what we are used to considering to be our greatest asset – our intellectual mind – is merely a toy compared to the vast power of our total mind.

In practice, this means that when we think we have an idea, our brain has already had that idea. *We* didn't actually come up with it. Instead, our intellect simply found it amidst the countless other ideas and options that our subconscious mind created outside our awareness. It's as if something in our brains navigates us through the everyday adventures of life and decides things for us before we can think about them, because our brains are always switched on. We have a deeper wisdom that's an intrinsic part of our operating system so that we don't have to make sense of everything intellectually.

It can be difficult to let go of our intellectual habit to try to understand and make sense of everything. After all, we've been doing it for most of our lives and for many, it's hard to fathom of an alternative to trying to logically think and analyze our way out of every problem. That alternative is trust – trust that everything is going to be okay even if we stop analyzing, obsessing, controlling, planning and figuring things out. As unintuitive and vague as this may sound, it really isn't that different to swimming. If we don't trust that the water will support us, we are likely to try to grasp the water and resist it, but this will only cause us to sink. We are only able to swim when we trust that the water will support us, which allows us to relax and work together with the water to keep ourselves afloat. It's the same way with our deeper intelligence – it will work for us, but only when we trust it and allow it to.

So rather than trying to force-think our way through our problems using the extremely limited instrument that our conscious mind is, we can instead rely on our deeper wisdom to be there for us. Simply trusting our deeper intelligence to guide us allows our thinking to settle down and our minds to clear. A cluttered mind interferes with our deeper (subconscious) intelligence and prevents us from tapping into our deeper sense of insights and wisdom.

In many ways, accessing our deeper wisdom is like

falling asleep – the harder we try to fall asleep, the more we struggle to do so. The only way to fall asleep is to prepare the conditions so that the state of sleep can happen. In other words, we can only *allow* ourselves to fall asleep, we cannot *make* ourselves fall asleep. And in any situation, just like with falling asleep, we simply need to get out of our own heads to tap into our full potential – i.e. accessing our deeper wisdom and allowing the answers to come.

When left alone, our minds tend to perform remarkably well. Throughout history, spiritual teachers have called this "the kindness of the design" and "our inbuilt intelligence" or "the god within", and they all point to the same realization: if we can simply let go of the wheel of our minds and let it self-correct, it will automatically regain its balance and guide us with remarkable reliability. The only real impediment to our deeper wisdom is ourselves; our lack of trust and our need to feel in control. The fact of the matter is, we've never been in control and we never will be. The sooner we understand this, the sooner we can stop interfering with the autopilot that already knows how to get us to our destination.

Our Inbuilt Guidance System

If everything is made up of thought, then how do we know which thoughts to follow and which to ignore? And doesn't this mean that we can justify *anything* as a by-product of thought? If we look into the past, this does indeed seem to be the case; human history is littered with wars, genocides, suicides, riots, abuse, discrimination, and all sorts of other insane acts – all because people believed their thinking.

Fortunately, there is a reliable way to distinguish between thoughts that stem from wisdom and those that lead us astray, sometimes causing us to do crazy things. We are all born with an inbuilt guidance system that lets us know when our thinking is guiding us wisely and when we're going off track. Our feelings are that guidance system.

Like many others, I have spent much of my life misinterpreting what my feelings were telling me. When I was afraid, I interpreted my thoughts to mean that I should either remove myself from the situation or fix it so it wasn't scary anymore. When I felt demotivated, I figured it meant that it wasn't the right goal for me or that I should wait until I was motivated again. When I was angry, I thought my feelings meant that things shouldn't be as they are and that someone someone was to blame for it or for how I was feeling. When I was excited and energized, I thought it was because I had something exciting to look forward to.

What I didn't understand was that my feelings weren't telling me anything about my circumstances; my feelings weren't warning me about my goals, my finances, or my abilities. Instead, I was being warned about the quality of my thinking. Allow me to elaborate: if the only thing we can feel stems purely from our thinking, then our feelings cannot (reliably) tell us anything about the outside world, they can only inform us of the quality of our thinking. This was a total game changer for me. What I realized was that when I felt scared, demotivated, or angry, it had literally *nothing* to do with my circumstances and *everything* to do with my state of mind. In other words, I didn't need to do anything about my circumstances to feel better.

By realizing that the feelings we have are caused by the quality of our thinking, we understand that when we feel bad, it's because our thinking is distorted and unclear, and we therefore cannot trust our feelings to guide us. As a result, rather than stopping or changing paths, our best course of action is to push through and continue with the plan that we devised from a clear state of mind.

For instance, now when I feel nervous in front of a large crowd, I smile inside and relax because I know that my nervousness has nothing to do with the crowd – I'm just feeling my thinking and whatever meaning I've given the situation. Another example is when I find myself in the middle of an argument. All I need to do is be aware of how I'm feeling. If I start to feel angry or uncomfortable, I remind myself that the argument itself is not causing any particular reaction from me but rather my thinking about the situation, the person or the topic. When I see that the only thing I'm ever reacting to is my own thinking allows me to trust my inner guidance to continue the conversation (in a constructive and controlled manner) or choose to remove myself from it. There are countless examples that I could list that all point to the same thing: since circumstances are neutral and don't have the ability to make me feel one way or another, whatever I'm feeling is only informing me of the quality of my thinking.

Although simply "staying in the game" may seem somewhat underwhelming on the surface, because it isn't a technique to make us instantly feel better, it points to our incredible inbuilt guidance system. The way this system works is that when we feel "low" (anxious, excited, fearful, envious, angry, frustrated, demotivated, etc), our inbuilt guidance system is telling us that we're not thinking straight and that we've slipped to a lower level of consciousness where our thoughts seem real. On the other hand, when we feel peaceful, calm, or joyful, it's an indication that our mind is uncluttered and we have clarity of thought.

	POSITIVE FEELING	NEGATIVE FEELING
What it feels like	Content, peaceful, loving, happy (but not excited or ecstatic)	Uncertain, anxious, restless, urgent, irritated, bored, stressed-out, uncomfortable, excited
What it means	You can trust your thinking	You CANNOT trust your thinking
Guide to action	You can trust your thinking to guide your behavior	Ignore all thoughts and simply keep going. Stick to the plan. Do NOT stop.

PICTURE 20 - Feelings of contentment, peace, and happiness let us know we can trust our thoughts. Feelings of uncertainty, anxiety, and urgency warn us that we cannot.

Our feelings serve as the middleman between our thoughts and actions, telling us whether we should act on those thoughts or not. Put another way, our feelings are an indicator that lets us know whether or not we can trust our thinking. This gives us a remarkably reliable way of navigating through our own wisdom.

> THOUGHT → FEELING → BEHAVIOR

PICTURE 21 - The key to changing our behavior is to realize what causes it in the first place.

It's important to notice that just because we feel off doesn't mean we should stop what we are doing. To the contrary – it generally means we should ignore our thinking and stay the course. In fact, the only times our emotional states seem to correlate with our level of performance is in situations where we *believe* that we need to feel a certain way in order to successfully complete a particular task.

Thus, when we are feeling low, we should distrust everything our mind is telling us and proceed with what we were doing or planning on doing. With a negative state of mind, we are clearly not thinking straight and any idea that occurs to us in that state should be treated with suspicion.

If that is the case, when *should* we deviate from a set plan? The only sensible time to deviate from a plan is when we are calm and peaceful but still want to change course. If, for instance, you feel calm and good about changing your speech, quitting your job, or cancelling your workout, it's usually an exceptionally reliable signal that you can trust your thinking. Learn to let your inner navigation system guide you.

At its most fundamental level, how we feel is an indication of the type of thinking we have going on in the moment. In other words, whether our thinking is fear or love based. Feelings of fear, anxiety, anger, cravings, and urgency are all examples of feelings based in fear. Fear is the ultimate mind distorter; it narrows our vision so that we only see that which is right in front of us and makes us blind to everything else that is going on around us and inside us. On the other hand, a calm, peaceful, or joyful feeling lets us know that our feelings aren't fear-based. Rather than acting from a place of desperation, we operate from a place of possibility. We aren't acting from a place of desperation, but from a place of possibility. It is ultimately to help us distinguish between fear-based thoughts and love-based thoughts that our inbuilt guidance system was created.

No doubt you have already been using this inbuilt guidance system from time to time. There are two reasons most of us don't use it more often. Firstly, we haven't learned to recognize when we are in a low mood. When we don't recognize our low mood, we don't realize that we cannot trust our thinking, and we consequently end up buying into our contaminated thinking. At times it can be easy to notice a low mood, but more often than not, when we are in a low mood we don't realize it. It can be subtle – a general irritability or heaviness, for example – but it can rapidly manifest itself into poor decision making and behavior if we overlook the warning signs.

The second obstacle to using our inbuilt guidance system more is that we haven't learned to trust that our feelings really do guide us. When we get caught up in a negative emotion – such as fear, anger, or apathy – it can be treacherously easy to find reasons to justify that emotion and look for the culprit in our circumstances, to pull back rather than lean in and keep going. But all that generally does is reinforce the outside-in illusion and make the negative feeling stronger, which leads to poor choices and bad behavior. Once we learn to trust that our negative feelings are just a reminder that our thinking is steering us off course, we can simply stop taking our thoughts so seriously. That's it. We don't have to resist the thoughts, fight them, or try to change them – we can simply take them for what they are: momentary illusions that will soon pass on their own. Here are some common indicators to help you notice your low mood:

- You feel uncertain or indecisive
- Your sense of humor has disappeared or you feel irritated
- You have a sense of urgency or an all-or-nothing mentality
- You just feel "off" (heavy, apathetic, listless, etc.)

The point isn't to obsess constantly how you are feeling (that would just be another form of added thinking), but rather to help you catch yourself when you are feeling low and recognize that the feeling stems from your thinking and not your circumstances. This will allow you to steer past the many well camouflaged, self-created landmines that your low mood has plotted in your path, because you will know to ignore whatever thoughts you may be having and keep doing what you had planned until your mood improves.

This points to an insight that firefighters know intrinsically: how we feel is not an indicator of how well we will perform. A firefighter might be feeling sad, lonely, demotivated, or insecure at any given moment, but once it's time to run into a burning building, he knows that none of his feelings can interfere with his ability to do his job. The same is true for you and me – if we sit on the sidelines and wait to feel better, we're going to miss out on countless opportunities and experiences to serve, perform, and excel.

>   **Example 1:** You get into an argument with your spouse because – once again – they've left certain chores around the house undone that you believe they should have taken care of. Knowing that any anger or resentment is just the result of your state of mind rather than the actions of your partner will help you keep a cooler head. After some time has passed and you feel calm and secure about the issue, you can then make an informed decision on how to handle the situation.
>
>   **Example 2:** You wake up feeling tired and wonder if you should skip today's workout at the gym. Your low-energy state is telling you that you can't trust your thinking. Simply ignore your thinking and go do your regular workout. *(However, when it IS time to change things up and skip a workout, the feeling will be direct, immediate, and resolute – i.e. no intellectual thought or reasoning is involved. You simply won't go to the gym.)*
>
>   **Example 3:** You are nervous and stressed about your presentation before an important meeting and wonder whether you should try to postpone it until later when you feel more confident. The nervous and stressed feelings reveal that you can't trust your thinking. Ignore your thinking and proceed with the meeting.
>
>   **Example 4:** You are at work, when you suddenly have a calm, certain feeling that you are going to quit your job and start your own online business. If the impulse is a calm feeling of certainty, it's a pretty reliable sign that you should at least consider trusting your gut and making the move. If, however, you feel anxious, excited, or restless about the idea, it's a sign to distrust your thinking on the matter and not do anything rash.

The point of these examples is to illustrate how our feelings always guide us in the right direction. When we don't understand the inside-out nature of our experience, we are likely to draw wrong conclusions that prevent us from living our life to its fullest. For instance, without the inside-out understanding it is easy to mistake a lack of motivation as a sign that we should stop and wait until we feel better or more inspired, because it seems to us that our feelings are telling us information about our progress or ability. However, if we only take action when we're in a high state of mind (feeling motivated, confident, and ready), we are likely to keep putting our project on hold every time we are not in a high state of mind. What an incredible waste of time and energy!

Rather than wait to feel good, we can just move ahead and take the next step. How good or bad we feel isn't relevant once we recognize those feelings are coming from our thinking. So the next time you find yourself in a low mood, simply distrust your thinking, not your actions, and keep going. It's only a matter of time before you mood elevates again.

Living from the Inside-Out

What makes the inside-out approach particularly unique and powerful is that it doesn't require techniques, strategies, routines, discipline, or willpower to have a significant positive impact on our lives. There is nothing that we need to do – we only need to understand that our thoughts create our perception of reality and that our mind automatically performs optimally when we stop interfering with it. Perhaps the best part about the inside-out paradigm is that even a basic understanding transforms our lives on all levels, not just where we remember to apply it. It really is the solution to almost all of life's problems, because by seeing the role of thought as the creator of our experience our problems either disappear or our perspective of our problems changes and the mountains shrink back into molehills. When we simply allow our mood to change, our problems solve themselves.

Let's now turn to what living from the inside-out might look like. I say might, because this is what I see and experience, but it might not be what you see. Thus, what follows are not prescriptions for how you or anyone else should behave or live, but simply some ways in which we can show up in the world with a sense of lightness, authenticity, courage, and ease.

When we understand the inside-out nature of reality, we can simply... go all in

When we understand that there is never anything on the line except for whatever meaning we've given it in our heads, we are free to put everything we have on the line and give it our best shot. Rather than hesitating, resisting, and looking around for better options, we can simply jump into life's challenges with both feet. When we are one foot in and one foot out, we cannot fully connect with life. However, when we go all in, not only does life become more fun, but we also tend to become more present in the moment and have more resources available to us to deal with whatever is in front of us.

Simply by going all in, we become better husbands,

wives, parents, friends, leaders, colleagues, neighbors and team mates. In the process, we tend to experience and enjoy life more richly, more directly, and more authentically. Instead of saying "ok, I'll give it a try" and dipping one toe into the water, we can yell "hell yes!" and jump in with both feet.

When we understand the inside-out nature of reality, we can simply... show up empty handed

When we are full of expectations and beliefs about a situation, it's easy to end up lost in our heads rather than being fully present in the moment. Every time we do something the same way we've done it before, it somehow feels less fresh and less magical, because we feel as though we know everything that is to come. However, once we see that our conceptual thinking – which is just a rehash of our past experiences and knowledge rather than anything new – isn't helping us and we learn to trust our deeper sense of wisdom, we no longer have to bring our conceptual thinking to all situations. We can simply show up empty handed and curious, trusting our deeper wisdom to guide us to the answers when we need them.

When we understand the inside-out nature of reality, we can simply... find our own answers

When we look outside for answers, we only reinforce the outside-in illusion that we live in an objective reality that creates our experience. But once we understand that we are fundamentally incapable of experiencing actual reality, searching for answers in our own mind-created illusions no longer seems like a smart place to look. So rather than blindly accept the advice, example, or strategy of someone else for our own unique situation, we can simply look inside to see what makes sense for us.

Looking inside means that we don't have to do things the way others have done them. We can trust our unique wisdom in the moment to do things our way. This wisdom usually manifests itself in nudges, prompts, realizations, inspirations, and insights that have a sense of direction and a surprising obviousness to them. And the more we act on our wisdom and inspiration, the more we open up to more wisdom and inspiration. As we expand into life, the more our life expands – simply because we know where to look.

When we understand the inside-out nature of reality, we can simply... embrace the flow of our experience

When we understand that thought naturally ebbs and flows and that we have no control over it, we are freed of the task of trying to change others or to fix or avoid our low states of mind. We see that no matter how things may appear, it's only our temporary personal version of reality that we can simply leave be. This understanding allows us to simply get on with our lives regardless of how we are feeling.

We can feel angry without lashing out, insecure without pulling back, and embarrassed without hiding. Embracing the ebb and flow of our experience allows our lives to become easier, simpler, lighter, and more fun. We start to see that we don't need to feel motivated to go for a jog, inspired to work on our novel, or confident to ask someone out. Whatever we feel is just a reflection of our thinking and not reality. This means we can stop running from uncomfortable experiences and embrace all of them, because we know that it's all made up and will change all on its own, without us having to do anything about it.

When we understand the inside-out nature of reality, we can simply... explore and experiment

When we realize that happiness – like every other emotion – is random, we are free to explore and experiment, because we no longer have a happiness we need to protect or achieve. We can simply follow our curiosity and wisdom to do what we want to do. We don't need to know every step along the way or the probability of success before starting – we can simply take the first step, trusting that the next step will appear in due time.

This allows us to show up in the world in a totally different way – after all, when we are enjoying the journey, we tend to find ourselves in less of a rush to arrive. And when we see that our happiness and wellbeing aren't at stake, it doesn't make sense to try to coerce ourselves into wanting what we don't truly want or doing what we don't really want to do. Simply by following what we are already genuinely motivated to do, be, and have tends to lead us to finding a way to do, be, or have it. Thus, the only thing we need to discover is what we genuinely want to do, and the only place to look is to follow our curiosity.

When we understand the inside-out nature of reality, we can simply... be guided by our feelings

When we realize that there is a deeper wisdom to our feelings, we can receive and embrace them in a new way. Rather than trying to minimize our negative feelings or interpret them as a sign that something is wrong with us or our circumstances, we can see that our feelings are the barometer of the quality of our thinking in the moment. This enables us to navigate our lives with remarkable reliability, clarity, and ease, as our feelings will tell us when our thinking is steering us off course. And when the warning signal goes off, all we need to do is take our thinking a little less seriously and carry on with our lives. It's that simple.

When we understand the inside-out nature of reality, we can simply... just be ourselves

The only thing that prevents us from seeing that we are already more than enough for any challenge or opportunity is our own thinking. In fact, each of us is perfectly suited to function as a human being on this planet. It's what we were made for. Whatever imperfection, damage, lack, or fault we identify in ourselves is simply a temporary illusion created by our minds. Seeing this allows us to stop trying to be something we're not and simply relax into ourselves.

Fortunately, there's nothing we can do to be ourselves. We are authentic when we aren't trying to be something else. Trying to be authentic makes us less authentic. We can't be something we're not, but we can interfere with our true nature and make ourselves feel inadequate and insecure. As we let go of the need to live up to some idealized concept of self, we naturally bring our true essence forward and express our true nature in the world. So rather than trying to manage our thinking and manipulate the world of form, we can just be ourselves and express what is in our hearts in each moment knowing that it is enough.

When we understand the inside-out nature of reality, we can simply... connect deeply with others

When we see that we all live in separate thought-created realities, it becomes fascinating to hear and see what others are experiencing. We can become curious over things we would have previously considered boring or mundane. We can hang out with and talk to people we would normally avoid. What are they seeing and experiencing? What meaning have they given to particular thoughts and circumstances? What wisdom do they have to share?

We begin to realize that we all are one; inextricable parts of the same system. Whether people see it or not, we all generate our experience from the inside-out and we are all manifestations of the same spiritual energy. We see that the only thing that prevents us from connecting with others is our own thinking. This allows us to listen to others with more curiosity and presence, and we begin to feel a natural empathy and understanding for what others are dealing with in their lives.

When we understand the inside-out nature of reality, we can simply... see the innocence in everyone

When we realize the inside-out nature of reality, it becomes apparent that even people we consider "evil" are simply acting based on an innocent misunderstanding: that they believe they cannot be happy unless they go through with whatever terrible thing it is that they're doing. In other words, thinking appears in their head and they believe it, which leads them to adopt a "the end justifies the means" philosophy. The irony is that their happiness and mental wellbeing were never at stake and they were simply acting based on an illusion.

While seeing the evil in others as just an innocent misunderstanding may seem radical and scary at first, the truth of it becomes apparent when we look back at our own "low lights" and see that in each of those moments it seemed like a good idea – on some level – to take our bad mood out on the waitress, eat someone's lunch from the fridge, or worse. We've all done selfish, ill-considered, mean things along the way – simply because we believed our thinking that told us that it was the only way to feel good, justified, or safe. The instance we see the truth of this about ourselves, we see it about others too. And thus, instead of judging others, we can stop taking things personally and start to feel understanding, empathy, and compassion toward them. Ultimately, all "evil" is is us taking our thoughts too seriously and acting on them.

Closing Words

We are at the end of our journey together, and I hope this book has helped you see a glimpse of the inside-out nature of life for yourself, because a single glimpse is all you need to transform your experience of life forever. Once you've peeked behind the curtain, you can never go back to the way you saw things before – it simply doesn't make any sense to go back. You now know first-hand how the system works, which means you can finally align with how things actually are – with reality.

When we align ourselves with what is and realize that however we feel about it is just our own temporary mental creation, we can let go of mental coping strategies and just ride the wave of human experience, whatever it may be. Whether it's morbid thoughts of death, intense feelings of worry, terror and rage, or bizarre sexual urges, we can simply see them as thought and allow them to pass through us. The less we try to avoid, fix, or resist our feelings and instead allow the energy of life to move through us, the more effortless and beautiful our lives become. When we let go of our imaginary steering wheel, we free up an immense amount of energy that allows us to experience life more deeply, follow our curiosity to create new things, and make mistakes we've never made before.

Now, just because we know where our experience comes from doesn't mean that we won't occasionally lose sight of it and get caught up in our thinking. It happens to everyone, no matter how long we've been with this understanding. So if it happens to you, don't be too hard on yourself. We're all doing the best we can with the thinking we have in the moment. It is the human condition that we are constantly flowing back and forth between the physical and the spiritual dimensions of being human. That's simply the nature of the game. Like yin and yang, the physical and spiritual realms may seem like opposites but in reality, they are complementary and interdependent, each giving life to the other.

Although I have done my very best to explain human reality to you, what you have learned in this book is simply the tip of the iceberg, constrained by the limitations of my own understanding of the topic and my ability to communicate it to you. Yet if all this book achieved was to awaken you to the inside-out nature of your experience and the incredible reliability of your inner wisdom, it will have been a success.

As my parting thought to you, I want you to know that you are already perfect, whole, and mentally healthy exactly as you are. Whatever it is that you think you are lacking or that is causing you pain is, in fact, only a thought that you've given meaning to. Everything you experience is through your thinking, and sometimes you feel pain or fear because you think painful or scary thoughts. But rather than try to fix your thinking, you can simply look past it toward your deeper wisdom and the peace and joy that are always there, under the surface, just waiting to shine through. Once you realize that you are the answer you have been looking for all this time, there is nothing more for you to do – you will finally realize that you are free, and everything will simply fall into place.

"What we see as death, empty space, or nothingness is only the trough between the crests of this endlessly waving ocean. It is all part of the illusion that there should seem to be something to be gained in the future, and that there is an urgent necessity to go on and on until we get it. Yet just as there is no time but the present, and no one except the all-and-everything, there is never anything to be gained—though the zest of the game is to pretend that there is." –Alan Watts

Acknowledgements

This book took over 18 months to write and lays the foundation for all my coaching work with people from various professions, cultures and backgrounds.

This book is autobiographical in the sense that it is exactly what I wish someone would have told me when I was 20. It just turned out that it took me 42 years to get there.

I am incredibly grateful to all the people who have supported, loved, indulged and put up with me over the course of the past 40+ years. There are far too many of you to even think of listing here. Simply know that I am the person that I am today because of you.

I feel the need to mention two people in particular for their efforts and support in enabling this book to be what it is:

Kristie Stenhouse – my loving wife and editor. Your countless hours of work and insights on this book are only surpassed by your support for my work. I thank the heavens that you are in my corner - on this project and every other life's endeavor. I love you.

Marko Myllyluoma – I am forever grateful for your insightful feedback, the stunning cover design and for creating a professional layout for the book. Thank you, my friend.

Here is a short and no doubt incomplete list of all the people who supported, guided and loved me in the process of creating this book: Chris Rowell, Bruce Fleming, Ben Nothnagel, Kari Rytkönen, Steve M Nash, Juha Rajuvaara, Donal Crotty, Jody Wren, Mark Stenhouse, Toni Hyyryläinen, Niko Leppänen, Krista Kosonen, Pekka Punkari, Pauliina Himanka. Words cannot express how much your support means to me. Thank you from all my heart.

I am also indebted to the many incredible people who have made this spiritual journey before me and left signposts along the way so that others like me might find their way there, too. Here are the people whose work has most impacted me and the creation of this book: Sydney Banks, Michael Neill, Alan Watts, George Pransky, Jack Pransky, Garret Kramer, Eckhart Tolle

My sincerest thanks to everyone who helped in the creation of this book and to everyone who took this journey with me. May this book help light the way for the next group of spiritual seekers and bring about more peace and joy in the world by pointing people in the only direction that matters - inside.

Inward and upward,
Antti Vanhanen
In Helsinki
November 11th, 2017

Contact details for information and inquiries about being coached by me: www.devilinagoodman.com

Made in the USA
Monee, IL
15 September 2022